Good co[...]
Sylvia P.

L'Chaim + Bon Appétit
Mildred L. [...]

KOSHER CAJUN COOKBOOK

KOSHER CAJUN COOKBOOK

By Mildred L. Covert
and Sylvia P. Gerson

Illustrations by Alan Gerson

Pelican Publishing Company

GRETNA 1987

Library of Congress Cataloging-in-Publication Data

Covert, Mildred L.
    Kosher Cajun cookbook.

    Includes index.
    1. Cookery, Jewish.   2. Cookery, American –
Louisiana style.   I. Gerson, Sylvia P.   II. Title.
TX724.C68   1987   641.5′676   87-21110
ISBN 0-88289-651-2

Manufactured in the United States of America
Published by Pelican Publishing Company, Inc.
1101 Monroe Street, Gretna, Louisiana 70053

To our husbands, Lester and Dave,
who patiently savored and enjoyed
our Kosher Cajun recipes.

Contents

Foreword

What does kosher mean? The root of this Hebrew word means "properly prepared." When used in connection with food, kosher has come to mean "ritually proper." It does not describe a kind of menu, cuisine, or style of cooking. Kosher food fulfills the requirements of the dietary laws enumerated in Leviticus 11.

The Bible repeats the verse "Thou shalt not seethe a kid in its mother's milk" three times (Exod. 23:19, 34:26, and Deut. 14:21). The age-old Hebrew practice of separating milk products from meat products arises from this biblical injunction. This system of separation dictates that no meat or foods containing meat or its by-products be cooked, prepared, served, or eaten with milk or foods containing milk or its by-products.

Food that is neither meat nor milk is often called "pareve" (neutral) and can be eaten at any time with any meal. All vegetables as well as pure vegetable and mineral products are considered pareve. Types of fish specified in Leviticus and eggs from the fowl listed in this section of the Bible are also considered pareve and can be enjoyed at all meals.

Many reasons are advanced for observing the dietary rules of Judaism. Traditionalists believe that these laws were divinely ordained to help keep us a holy people. Others add that practicing the restrictions is hygienically wise. There are those who stress the spiritual value of the discipline involved, while some modernists maintain that the laws should be observed in order to perpetuate Jewish identity.

Instilling holiness as a regulating principle – not simply an abstract ideal – in our daily lives remains the primary reason for adherence to the laws. They train us in the mastery of our appetites; they accustom us to restraining the growth of desire and the disposition to consider the pleasure of eating and drinking the end of man's existence. However, all would no doubt agree that the laws of kashruth have also

9

been a significant factor in forming the unique character of the Jewish home. By means of these rules, religion enters the kitchen and accompanies the family to the table, designating it an altar of G-d.

Regarding the consumption of fish, Leviticus states "These shall ye eat of all that are in the water, whatsoever hath fins and scales" (Lev. 11:9). Thus shellfish, shrimp, lobster, crabs, turtles, eels, clams, and other scavenger fish cannot be eaten. Hence Cajun cooking, which has many of the above as its basic ingredients, has heretofore been denied the kosher palate.

With great culinary skill and ingenuity, Sylvia Gerson and Mildred Covert—members of Congregation Beth Israel in New Orleans—have succeeded uniquely and creatively in making accessible the traditional flavors of Cajun cooking while adhering completely to the laws of kashruth.

RABBI JONAH GEWIRTZ
Beth Israel Congregation
7000 Canal Boulevard
New Orleans, Louisiana

Introduction

Louisiana is a land of many contrasts, enjoying the best of both worlds. Modern technology works its magic on the oil rigs off the coast of the mighty Mississippi River, while just a few miles away lie towns steeped in unchanged, century-old customs and traditions. This is Cajun country. Then there are the Cajuns themselves.

In 1755 refugees from Canada began arriving in south Louisiana after being exiled from Nova Scotia. Primarily farmers of French nationality, they were welcomed to the predominately French territory of Louisiana. They quickly settled and established farms along the bayous and fishing and trapping villages in the swamplands. With their own culture and traditions, they helped shape what is now known as Acadiana. Indian inhabitants of the region, unable to pronounce "Acadians," dubbed them Cajuns. And they have remained, with their Cajun mystique and their unique language and culture, and prospered in southern Louisiana.

The best way to become acquainted with the Cajun country is to take a tour from New Orleans to Lafayette, the "official" capital of Acadiana. As you travel along Highway 90, the original route that predates interstate expressways, you will encounter many traditions, stories, and customs. You will hear a distinctly different music – the fiddlers and their "fais do-do." You will enjoy a never-ending country festival exhibiting the arts and crafts of the natives. It is perhaps the most colorful area in Louisiana. And above all, you will be introduced to the world of Cajun cooking.

Cajun cooking, we believe, can best be described as a close relative to the sophisticated Creole cooking. But although Creole and Cajun cuisines sometimes overlap, we readily recognize the differences. Cajun food is more down-to-earth and simpler, but it is hearty and possesses a fiery gusto. One might say it is the "soul food" of the French-Canadian descendants.

11

Kosher cooking, like Cajun cooking, has adapted to its surroundings. As more and more Jewish immigrants came to America and adjusted to the new land, they adopted not only the country and its customs but the food as well. They made use of what was available, but at all times they adhered to the Kashruth (the Jewish Dietary Laws) with its restrictions and Biblical injunctions. Kosher cooking was no longer stereotyped.

As creative cooks who had successfully invented Kosher Creole cooking, we thought the time had come to introduce still another fusion of ethnic cuisines – the Kosher and the Cajun. To that end we present these tantalizing, Kashruth-approved delicacies from our Louisiana Kosher-Cajun kitchen.

MILDRED L. COVERT
and
SYLVIA P. GERSON

KOSHER CAJUN COOKBOOK

Lafayette
SOUPS, GUMBOS, AND BISQUES

Lafayette, the Cajun capital of Louisiana, can be reached as one travels along Louisiana Highway 90. It lies in the heart of southwestern Louisiana. Acadians from Nova Scotia first settled there in the 1750s. The city was laid out as Vermilionville in 1824; in 1884, the name was changed to Lafayette. This is the most colorful area of Acadiana, where tourists are introduced to the many traditions, stories, customs and life styles, the distinctive architecture, and the unique recipes of the Cajuns. It is here in the heart of Acadiana that one feels the pulse of the Cajun Country.

Lafayette is a city that represents Louisiana's past, present, and future. One can go back in time by visiting an Acadian village where a bit of the past has been preserved and recreated. Authentic Cajun cabins are furnished with arts and crafts handmade by the area's skilled artisans. Tourists interested in the present can play the horses at Evangeline Downs. The more daring can take a pirogue down Cypress Lake and perhaps catch a glimpse of an alligator or listen to Cajun fiddlers. Present-day Lafayette boasts a newly built Cajundome which can seat 14,000 people. For those interested in the future, Lafayette is the heart of Louisiana's petroleum industry, an industry that spawns the technological wonders awaiting us in the twenty-first century.

Past, present, or future, Acadians can always find an excuse to eat, drink, and dance, and festivals are an integral part of their lives. In Lafayette, the Festivals Acadiens is the granddaddy of all Louisiana festivals, with seven festivals rolled into one.

The Festivals Acadiens highlights gumbos, etouffées, and jambalayas, which always feature hot, spicy flavors. This distinct flavor can be created in the Kosher kitchen. The Kosher cook, like the Cajuns and tourists, takes her fun and food seriously. They all agree, "Laissez les bon temps rouler!" or "Let the good times roll!"

SOUPS, GUMBOS, AND BISQUES

Acadian Artichoke Soup *(Conventional)*
Alcée's Artichoke Soup *(Microwave)*
Big Daddy's Fish Soup *(Conventional)*
Bon Temps Turkey Soup *(Conventional and Processor)*
Bubbie's Bouillabaisse *(Microwave and Processor)*
Cajundome Soup *(Conventional)*
Coon-ass Gumbo *(Conventional)*
Festival Fish Soup *(Microwave and Conventional)*
Gittel's Gumbo *(Microwave)*
Grandpère's Onion Soup *(Microwave)*
Lafayette Lentil Soup *(Microwave and Conventional)*
Oprah's Okra Soup *(Conventional)*
Poulet Gumbo *(Conventional)*
Rebbitzen's Red Bean Soup *(Microwave)*
Sal's Salmon Soup *(Conventional)*
Tzibel Soup *(Conventional)*
Vermilion Vegetable Soup *(Microwave and Processor)*
Zayde's Zucchini Bisque *(Conventional and Processor)*

ACADIAN ARTICHOKE SOUP

1 bunch shallots, chopped
3 bay leaves, crumbled
pinch of thyme
cayenne pepper to taste
4 tbsp. pareve margarine
2 tbsp. flour
1 10½-oz. can kosher
   condensed chicken soup

1 14-oz. can artichoke
   hearts, chopped
3 sprigs of parsley, chopped
½ cup nondairy creamer
salt to taste
dash of nutmeg

Sauté shallots, bay leaves, thyme, and cayenne pepper in pareve margarine. Add flour and stir well. Add chicken soup and simmer 15 minutes. Add artichoke hearts and parsley. Simmer another 10 minutes. Remove from heat, stir in nondairy creamer. Add salt and nutmeg. Serves four.

ALCÉE'S ARTICHOKE SOUP

½ cup pareve margarine
1 cup chopped onions
½ cup chopped shallots
2 cloves garlic, chopped
¼ tsp. thyme
1 bay leaf
½ tsp. garlic salt
½ tsp. ground white pepper
½ tsp. ground cayenne
   pepper

½ tsp. ground black pepper
¼ tsp. crushed basil
¼ tsp. Tabasco sauce
2 14-oz. cans artichoke
   hearts, drained and
   chopped
1 10½-oz. can kosher
   condensed chicken soup
1 10½-oz. can kosher
   pareve mushroom soup

In a 4-cup glass bowl, combine pareve margarine, onions, shallots, and garlic. Microwave on High for 3 to 4 minutes or until soft but not brown. In a 3-quart casserole, combine sautéed vegetables and all the remaining ingredients. Cover. Microwave on 70 percent power for 10 to 12 minutes or until almost boiling. Let stand 10 minutes before serving. Serves four to six.

BIG DADDY'S FISH SOUP

2 lbs. fish heads, bones and
   trimmings
3 cups water
1 cup dry white wine
2/3 cup sliced onions
2 celery tops with leaves
3 sprigs parsley
1 bay leaf
1/4 tsp. dried thyme
1/2 cup olive oil
2 lbs. each of 3 kinds of
   fish fillets, such as
   flounder, red snapper,
   redfish, trout, mackerel,
   cut into 2-inch pieces
1 cup coarsely chopped
   fresh tomato pulp (about
   1 lb. tomatoes, peeled,
   seeded, and gently
   squeezed)

1 tbsp. finely chopped fresh
   parsley
1 tsp. finely chopped garlic
1/2 tsp. dried oregano,
   crumbled
1/8 tsp. powdered saffron or
   crumbled saffron threads
1 tsp. salt
freshly ground black pepper
2 tbsp. finely chopped fresh
   parsley
1 tbsp. freshly grated lemon
   peel

In 6-quart soup pot, combine fish heads, bones, and trimmings with water and wine. Bring to a boil over high heat, skimming off any foam that rises to the surface. Add the onions, celery tops, parsley sprigs, bay leaf, and thyme and return stock to a boil. Reduce the heat and simmer uncovered for 20 minutes. Strain the stock through a fine sieve into a deep bowl or saucepan, pressing down hard with a spoon on the fish trimmings and vegetables to extract their juices before discarding them.

Heat the olive oil in a heavy 4- to 5-quart pot until a light haze forms over it. Brown the fish in the oil over moderately high heat for only 2 or 3 minutes on each side. With a bulb baster, remove all but 2 or 3 tablespoons of oil. Stir the saffron into the strained fish stock and add to it the tomatoes, 1 tablespoon of the chopped parsley, the garlic, the oregano, the salt, and a few grindings of pepper. Bring the soup to a simmer, stirring gently; then reduce heat, cover, and cook for 5 to 8 minutes or until the fish is firm to the touch and flakes easily when pierced with a fork. Do not overcook. Taste and season with more salt and pepper, if desired. Sprinkle with the remaining chopped parsley and the grated lemon peel. Serves six to eight.

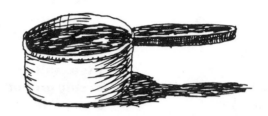

BON TEMPS TURKEY SOUP

1 turkey carcass
2 onions, cut in half
3 ribs celery with tops, cut
   into thirds
2 carrots, cut into thirds
3 cups fresh corn kernels
   cut from cob (about 5
   ears), reserve cobs
1 bay leaf

pinch thyme
pinch basil
12 cups water
1 tbsp. salt
1 tsp. black pepper
1 tsp. Worcestershire sauce
¼ tsp. Tabasco sauce
pinch curry powder
¼ cup dry sherry

In an 8-quart pot, place turkey carcass, onions, celery, carrots, corn cobs, bay leaf, thyme, and basil. Add water and bring to a boil. Cover and simmer 1½ hours, stirring occasionally. Strain and return stock to pot.

Remove onions, celery, carrots, and 1 cup raw corn from strainer and place in a food processor fitted with a steel blade. Pulse on and off until vegetables are puréed. Add 2 cups stock and pulse twice to mix well. Return puréed vegetables to pot containing the stock. Add remaining 2 cups corn and cook for 30 minutes. Add salt, pepper, Worcestershire sauce, Tabasco, curry powder, and sherry. Stir well before serving. Serves ten.

BUBBIE'S BOUILLABAISSE

heads and bones from
   redfish and red snapper
1 slice lemon
½ tsp. thyme
1 bay leaf
1 tbsp. chopped parsley
4 cups water
1 tsp. ground thyme
¼ cup parsley, ground
1 bay leaf, ground
3 cloves garlic, ground
¼ tsp. ground cloves
2 tbsp. olive oil
2 lbs. red snapper fillets,
   cut into 2-inch pieces

2 lb. redfish fillets, cut into
   2-inch pieces
2 tbsp. olive oil
1 cup chopped onions
⅔ cup sherry
1 8-oz. can tomato sauce
½ lemon, cut into very thin
   slices
½ tsp. garlic salt
½ tsp. ground white pepper
½ tsp. ground red pepper
½ tsp. ground black pepper
¼ tsp. dry mustard
¼ tsp. Tabasco sauce
pinch ground saffron

In a 2-quart bowl, combine fish heads and bones, lemon slice, ½ teaspoon thyme, 1 whole bay leaf, 1 tablespoon parsley, and 4 cups water. Mix well and cover. Microwave on High for 10 to 12 minutes, or until boiling. Allow mixture to boil on High an additional 3 minutes. Let stand, covered, for 10 minutes.

In a food processor fitted with a steel knife, combine remaining teaspoon thyme, ¼ cup parsley, 1 bay leaf, garlic, and cloves with 2 tablespoons olive oil. Pulse 4 or 5 times, until mixture resembles a soft paste.

Spread the paste over the fish fillets. In a 5-quart casserole, combine remaining 2 tablespoons olive oil and onions. Mix well. Microwave on High for 2 to 3 minutes, or until onions are softened. Add fish fillets and cover. Microwave on High for 2 minutes, turn, cover and microwave on High for 2 additional minutes. Remove fish fillets and set aside.

To the casserole add sherry, strained fish stock, tomato sauce, lemon slices, garlic salt, white pepper, red pepper, black pepper, and dry mustard. Cover. Microwave on High for 10 to 12 minutes, or until boiling. Add fish, Tabasco, and pinch of saffron. Cover. Microwave on High for 6 to 8 minutes or until fish is done. Let stand, covered, 10 minutes before serving. Serve over steamed rice. Serves eight.

CAJUNDOME SOUP

1 2-lb. beef soup bone, with
   meat
1 1-lb. veal bone
2 qts. water
1 clove garlic, crushed
2 bay leaves
1 tbsp. salt
2 sprigs parsley
2 stalks celery, with tops
1 onion, chopped

6 carrots, diced
3 turnips, diced
2 potatoes, peeled and cut
   into cubes
1 cup chopped tomatoes
½ cup fresh green beans,
   snapped in half, with tips
   and strings removed
salt and pepper to taste

Put soup bones, water, garlic, bay leaves, salt, parsley, celery, and onion in large soup pot. Cover and bring to a boil. Skim off scum, cover, reduce heat, and simmer for 4 hours. Remove bay leaves and bones, but reserve meat. Skim off excess fat and strain stock. Mix stock with meat, carrots, turnips, potatoes, tomatoes, and beans. Cover and simmer for an additional 30 minutes or until all vegetables are tender. Season to taste. Serves four.

COON-ASS GUMBO

1 3-lb. chicken, cut into
  pieces
4 cups water
¼ cup flour
¼ cup vegetable oil
1½ cups chopped onions
1½ cups chopped celery
½ cup chopped green
  pepper
½ cup chopped shallots
3 cloves garlic, pressed

¼ cup chopped fresh
  parsley
1 bay leaf
½ tsp. fresh thyme
¾ lb. kosher smoked
  sausage, thinly sliced
¼ tsp. cayenne pepper
1 tbsp. Worcestershire
  sauce
3 tsp. filé powder
salt and pepper to taste

Cook chicken in water until tender, skimming off fat and scum. Reserve stock and remove meat from bones.

In a heavy stock pot, heat oil and gradually add flour, stirring constantly to make a dark brown roux. Add onions, celery, green pepper, shallots, garlic, parsley, bay leaf, and thyme. Cook until tender, stirring often. Slowly add stock, stirring constantly. Add chicken meat.

In a skillet, fry sausage; drain off any drippngs and add sausage to gumbo. Cover and simmer for 1 hour, stirring occasionally. Add salt, pepper, cayenne, and Worcestershire sauce. Just before serving, sprinkle filé powder into gumbo. Serve over cooked rice. Serves six.

FESTIVAL FISH SOUP

2 stalks celery, diced
1 onion, chopped
3 tbsp. butter or margarine
4 medium-size potatoes,
  diced (about 4 cups)
2 bay leaves
1½ tsp. salt
½ tsp. Tabasco sauce
1 lb. redfish or red snapper
  fillets
1 10-oz. pkg. frozen French-
  cut green beans

1 10-oz. pkg. frozen green
  peas
1 tbsp. chopped fresh
  parsley (optional)
4 tbsp. sour cream
  (optional)
3 or 3½ cups water
  (depending on cooking
  method)

MICROWAVE METHOD: Combine celery, onion, and butter in a 4-quart casserole. Cover tightly. Microwave at 100 percent power for 3 minutes. Stir in 3 cups water, potatoes, bay leaves, salt, and Tabasco. Cover and microwave at 100 percent power for 12 minutes, stirring once.

Cut fish into 1-inch cubes. Add to soup mixture with beans and peas. Cover and microwave at 100 percent power for 15 minutes or until fish flakes easily, stirring once. Ladle into bowls and garnish each with chopped parsley and/or a tablespoon sour cream, if desired. Serves four.

CONVENTIONAL METHOD: Sauté celery and onion in butter or margarine until onion is transparent and celery is tender. Add 3½ cups water, potatoes, bay leaves, salt, and Tabasco. Heat to boiling. Reduce heat, cover, and simmer for 20 minutes. Add beans and peas and cook for 5 minutes, or until vegetables are thawed and soup is hot.

Cut fish into 1-inch cubes. Add to soup and cook 5 to 8 minutes longer or until fish flakes easily. Serve with parsley and/or sour cream garnish, if desired. Serves four.

GITTEL'S GUMBO

½ cup vegetable oil
½ cup all-purpose flour
1 cup chopped onions
½ cup chopped celery
½ cup chopped bell pepper
2 tbsp. chopped shallots
4 cloves garlic, chopped
2 cups chopped fresh okra
1 tbsp. Worcestershire
  sauce
¾ tsp. salt

½ tsp. ground white pepper
½ tsp. onion powder
½ tsp. cayenne pepper
½ tsp. paprika
½ tsp. dried thyme,
  crumbled
¼ tsp. ground black pepper
1½ qts. water
1 3- to 4-lb. chicken, cut
  into pieces
1 tbsp. filé powder

In a 4-cup glass bowl, combine flour and oil. Mix well. Microwave on High for 6 minutes or until roux is dark brown. Stir when there are 2 minutes left on the timer, then when there is 1 minute left, and again when there are 30 seconds left. Stir when timer counts to zero. If roux is not dark enough, continue to microwave on High for 30 seconds longer.

Add onions, celery, bell pepper, shallots, and garlic. Mix well. Microwave on High for 3 to 4 minutes or until vegetables are soft but not brown.

In a 5-qt. casserole, combine roux, okra, Worcestershire sauce, salt, white pepper, onion powder, cayenne pepper, paprika, crumbled thyme, and black pepper with water and chicken. Stir well and cover. Microwave on High for 15 minutes; then microwave on 50 percent power for 30 to 35 minutes or until chicken is done.

Skim off excess fat, add filé, and stir. Serve over steamed rice. Serves eight to ten.

GRANDPÈRE'S ONION SOUP

2 tbsp. melted pareve
  margarine
1 cup sliced onions
½ cup diced celery
½ tsp. thyme
½ tsp. sage

6 cups kosher beef broth
  (made with 3 beef
  bouillon cubes)
8 slices toasted French
  bread

Combine pareve margarine, onion, celery, thyme, and sage in a 2-quart glass casserole. Cover and microwave on High for 8 minutes or until vegetables are tender. Add broth, cover, and microwave on Medium (50 percent power) for 12 to 15 minutes or until hot.

Pour into bowls and place toasted bread slices on top. Serves eight.

LAFAYETTE LENTIL SOUP

6 slices Beef Frye, diced
2 onions, chopped
1 stalk celery, chopped
3 carrots chopped
1 lb. lentils, rinsed
2 10½-oz. cans condensed
  chicken soup, undiluted
¼ tsp. oregano

⅛ tsp. thyme
1 bay leaf
pinch cayenne pepper
1 hard-cooked egg, sieved,
  for garnish
3 or 4 cups hot water
  (depending on cooking
  method)

MICROWAVE METHOD: Combine Beef Frye, onions, celery, and carrots in a 4-quart casserole. Cover tightly. Microwave at 100 percent power for 8 minutes, stirring once. Add lentils, chicken soup, oregano, thyme, bay leaf, pepper, and 3 cups hot water. Cover and microwave at 100 percent power for 10 minutes. Stir well, cover, and microwave at 70 percent power for 30 minutes or until lentils are tender, stirring once or twice. Let stand 5 minutes. Remove bay leaf and serve soup garnished with egg. Serves six.

CONVENTIONAL METHOD: Sauté Beef Frye, onions, and celery in a large saucepan until onions are transparent and Beef Frye is crisp. Stir in carrots, lentils, chicken soup, oregano, thyme, bay leaf, pepper, and 4 cups water. Heat to boiling. Reduce heat, cover, and simmer for 40 minutes or until lentils are tender. Remove bay leaf and serve soup garnished with egg. Serves six.

OPRAH'S OKRA SOUP

2 lbs. okra
¼ cup vegetable oil (or enough to cover bottom of pot)
1 large onion, chopped
1 bell pepper, chopped

1 8-oz. can tomato sauce
1 clove garlic, minced
¼ tsp. black pepper
¼ tsp. cayenne pepper
salt to taste
10 cups water

Wash and dry okra; chop into thin, round slices. Heat oil in a large soup pot. When oil is hot, reduce fire to medium. Add okra and cover. Stir often to keep okra from sticking. When sticky substance has disappeared and okra is brownish, add onion, bell pepper, garlic, and seasonings. When onion and bell pepper have wilted a little, add water and tomato sauce. Cover and continue cooking for about 1 hour. Serves eight.

POULET GUMBO

1 qt. fresh okra, sliced
¼ cup vegetable oil
2 large onions, chopped
3 ribs celery, chopped
½ cup shallots, chopped
¼ cup parsley, chopped
3 qts. water

1 hen (about 6 lbs.), cut up
additional vegetable oil to
  cover bottom of large
  frying pan
½ tsp. cayenne pepper
salt and pepper to taste

Sauté sliced okra in ¼ cup of oil until golden brown. Add onions, celery, shallots, and parsley. Sauté until wilted. Add water; simmer until vegetables are well done.

In a heavy skillet, heat enough oil to cover bottom of pan. Brown chicken and add to vegetable mixture. Add cayenne pepper and salt and black pepper to taste. Cook on medium-low heat until chicken is tender, about 1 hour. Serves ten to twelve.

REBBITZEN'S RED BEAN SOUP

½ lb. ground beef
8 slices Beef Frye, cut up
1 medium onion, chopped
1 small green pepper,
  chopped
1 clove garlic, minced

1½ cups cubed kosher
  salami
1 lb. dried red beans,
  rinsed
6 cups hot water
¼ tsp. pepper

Place ground beef in a 1¼-quart casserole dish. Microwave, covered, on High for 2 to 4 minutes or until meat is no longer pink, stirring once to break meat apart. Drain and set aside.

In a 5-quart casserole dish combine Beef Frye, onion, green pepper, and garlic. Microwave on High for 6 to 7 minutes or until green pepper is tender, stirring once or twice.

Stir in ground beef, salami, red beans, water, and pepper; cover. Microwave on High for 15 to 20 minutes or until mixture is boiling, stirring once. Reduce power to 50 percent (Medium). Microwave for 1 to 1½ hours, or until beans are tender, stirring 3 or 4 times. Remove 1 cup beans, mash, and return to soup. For thinner soup, add 2 to 3 cups water. Serves ten to twelve.

SAL'S SALMON SOUP

3 tbsp. butter
¼ cup finely chopped
  celery
¼ cup finely chopped
  shallots, including tops
2 tbsp. flour

1 16-oz. can salmon, with
  liquid
1 tsp. salt
¼ tsp. cayenne pepper
2 cups hot milk

In the top of a double boiler, melt butter and sauté celery and shallots. Add flour and cook for 2 minutes, stirring so that flour will not lump. Add salmon with liquid and cook on low heat for an additional 5 minutes. Add salt, pepper, and hot milk; stir and serve. Serves four.

TZIBEL SOUP

4 onions
½ cup pareve margarine,
  melted
2 tbsp. flour
1 qt. chicken stock

½ tsp. thyme
½ tsp. sage
salt to taste
8 slices French bread

Slice onions very thin, add to melted pareve margarine, and cook slowly until tender but not brown. Add flour and blend well; then add hot chicken stock slowly, stirring constantly. Add thyme, sage, and salt to taste. Toast bread and spread with melted margarine. Place a slice of bread on each serving of soup. Serves eight.

VERMILION VEGETABLE SOUP

2 lbs. beef brisket
1 large onion
1 large potato
2 ribs celery
1½ qts. water
¾ tsp. salt
½ tsp. white pepper
½ tsp. onion powder
½ tsp. cayenne pepper
½ tsp. paprika
½ tsp. dried thyme
¼ tsp. freshly ground black
pepper

1 16-oz. can whole
tomatoes
1 cup chopped cabbage
3 carrots, chopped
1 large turnip, chopped
3 ribs celery, chopped
1 medium white onion,
chopped
1 medium potato, chopped
¼ cup chopped fresh
parsley
1½ cups fresh whole kernel
corn

In a 5-quart casserole, combine beef, whole onion, whole potato, celery ribs, water, and seasonings. Cover. Microwave on High for 20 minutes, then stir. Microwave on 50 percent power for 40 to 45 minutes or until meat is done.

Remove meat from pot. Separate meat from bone and chop into small pieces. Discard bone and skim fat. With slotted spoon remove vegetables from liquid. Place in food processor equipped with steel knife. Pulse 30 seconds or until vegetables are puréed. Return puréed vegetables to liquid.

Place cabbage, carrots, turnip, celery, onion, potato, parsley, and corn in food processor equipped with steel knife. Pulse 3 or 4 times just until vegetables are coarsely chopped. Add meat, tomatoes, and chopped vegetables to soup. Cover. Microwave on High for 30 to 35 minutes, or until vegetables are well done. Serves eight to ten.

ZAYDE'S ZUCCHINI BISQUE

1 medium onion, quartered
½ cup pareve margarine
1½ lbs. zucchini
2½ cups chicken stock
½ tsp. nutmeg

1 tsp. basil
1 tsp. salt
freshly ground black pepper
1 cup nondairy creamer

With the metal blade in place, add the onion to the beaker of the food processor. Process, turning on and off rapidly, until evenly chopped, about 5 seconds.

In a large saucepan, melt margarine and sauté onion until limp. With shredding disk, shred zucchini, using moderate pressure on the pusher. Add zucchini and chicken stock to the onion. Simmer, covered, for 15 minutes. Reinsert metal blade into processor and purée zucchini mixture in 2 batches, adding half the nutmeg, basil and salt and a few grinds of pepper to each batch. Combine batches, add the nondairy creamer, and stir until well mixed. Adjust seasoning to taste. Makes about 1½ quarts bisque.

St. Martinville
APPETIZERS, SALADS, AND DRESSINGS

Bienvenue. Welcome to St. Martin Parish and the small town of St. Martinville. It is located about thirteen miles east-southeast of Lafayette. As you approach St. Martinville, the majestic Evangeline Oak, probably the most famous tree in America, comes into view. It marks the landing place of the early settlers who traveled through the slow, peaceful waters of Bayou Teche. Acadians came not only from Nova Scotia but also from the Canary Islands and Spain, and some were refugees from France during the French Revolution. Even Creole families from New Orleans found their way to the Evangeline Oak. Natives of the area will tell you that the spreading branches of this stately oak are symbolic of the open arms that welcome all who come ashore.

As you stand beside this old tree, you can almost visualize the small boats filled with eager settlers gliding up the bayou and landing here. This spot was reputedly the meeting place of Emmeline Labiche and Louis Arcenaux. Their love story, which took place during the Acadian migration, was the inspiration for Henry Wadsworth Longfellow's immortal poem *Evangeline*.

Today, most of the residents of St. Martinville are descendants of those courageous early settlers. Here in the cradle of French culture and heritage, the old-world flavor is still quite apparent. Traditions and customs have been preserved. Many people still dress in Acadian costumes, and Cajun French is still spoken both at home and at work. When you talk to these people, listen to their music, learn about their culture, and partake of their special cooking – Cajun cooking. You will leave with an awareness of their warm hospitality and an understanding of their "joie de vivre" (joy of life).

APPETIZERS, SALADS AND DRESSINGS

Appetizers

Armand's Appetizer *(Conventional)*
Clotille's CraBalls *(Conventional)*
Delsey's Deviled Eggs *(Processor)*
Emmeline's Eggplant Dip *(Conventional and Processor)*
Evangeline's Eggplant Dip *(Microwave)*
Louie's Canapes *(Microwave)*
Lover's Lox *(Conventional)*
Mon Cher's Mold *(Processor)*
Pierre's Paté *(Processor)*
St. Martinville Salmon Spread *(Microwave and Conventional)*

Salads and Dressings

Becky's Black-eyed Pea Salad *(Processor)*
Becky's Salad Dressing *(Conventional)*
Chicken Salad Gabriel *(Conventional)*
Co-Co's Corn Salad *(Conventional)*
Co-Co's Dressing *(Conventional)*
Dudley's Coleslaw *(Processor)*
Malke's Macaroni Salad *(Conventional)*
Pirogue Potato Salad *(Conventional)*
René's Rice Salad *(Conventional)*
René's Mayonnaise *(Processor)*
Shrimp?! Salad *(Conventional)*
Shrimp?! Salad Dressing *(Conventional)*
Tzadik's Three-Bean Salad *(Conventional)*
Zack's Zucchini Salad *(Processor)*

ARMAND'S APPETIZER

¾ cup butter
4 cups chopped onions
⅓ cup chopped parsley
1 cup chopped bell pepper
½ lb. fresh mushrooms,
  chopped

½ tsp. powdered thyme
4 cloves garlic, crushed
¼ tsp. liquid crab boil
1 bay leaf
salt and pepper to taste
2 lbs. trout fillets

In a large skillet over medium heat, melt butter and sauté onions, parsley, bell pepper, and mushrooms for 10 to 15 minutes until soft but not browned. Add remaining ingredients (except trout) and simmer an additional 5 minutes. Add trout and cover with vegetable mixture. Cook over medium heat for 10 minutes or until fish is done. Stir well, breaking the fish into small pieces. Serve in chafing dish. Serves eight to ten.

CLOTILLE'S CRABALLS

2½ cups water
1 cup uncooked rice
1 tsp. salt
2 cups (about 8 oz.)
  shredded American
  cheese
¾ cup chopped onion
3 large cloves garlic,
  minced

1 tbsp. vegetable oil
¼ tsp. Tabasco sauce
2 cups deboned, skinned,
  and flaked smoked trout
3 eggs, beaten
2 cups bread crumbs
vegetable oil for deep frying

In a medium saucepan bring water to a boil. Stir in rice and salt and return to boiling. Reduce heat, cover, and simmer for 15 to 20 minutes or until rice is tender and water is absorbed. Remove from heat and stir in cheese. Set aside.

Sauté onion and garlic in 1 tablespoon oil until tender. Remove from heat and stir in Tabasco sauce and flaked smoked trout. Add rice mixture and stir well. Roll into 1-inch balls. Dip balls into beaten egg, then roll in bread crumbs.

Preheat vegetable oil in deep-fryer to 365° F. Fry balls for 2 to 3 minutes or until golden brown. Drain on absorbent paper towels. Serve hot. Makes about four dozen.

DELSEY'S DEVILED EGGS

6 boiled eggs
1 small sweet pickle
1 tbsp. tuna fish
¼ small bell pepper
1 small rib celery

2 tbsp. mayonnaise
1 tsp. Worcestershire sauce
¼ tsp. pepper
paprika or small sprigs of
    parsley (optional)

Cut boiled eggs in half lengthwise and carefully remove yolks. In food processor fitted with metal blade, place pickle, tuna fish, bell pepper, and celery. Process, turning on and off rapidly until finely chopped. Add egg yolks, mayonnaise, Worcestershire sauce and pepper. Pulse rapidly a few times until mixture is smooth. Stuff into egg whites. Garnish with sprinkling of paprika or small sprigs of parsley, if desired. Makes twelve.

EMMELINE'S EGGPLANT DIP

1 large eggplant
1 large onion
1 green bell pepper
1 clove garlic
½ cup olive oil

2 medium fresh tomatoes,
  peeled
salt and freshly ground
  black pepper to taste
2 tbsp. kosher white wine

Bake eggplant in preheated 400-degree oven until soft (about 45 minutes to 1 hour). Let cool. Place onion, bell pepper, and garlic in food processor fitted with metal blade. Process, turning on and off rapidly, until finely chopped. Sauté chopped onion, bell pepper, and garlic mixture in olive oil until vegetables are tender but not brown.

Peel and quarter eggplant. With the metal blade process eggplant and tomatoes until finely chopped. Mix the eggplant and tomatoes together with sautéed vegetables. Add seasonings and cook over medium heat until mixture is fairly thick. Remove from heat, add wine, and refrigerate. Serve well chilled with thinly sliced rye or pumpernickel bread. Makes about one pint.

EVANGELINE'S EGGPLANT DIP

1 large eggplant
¼ cup olive oil
½ cup minced onion
¼ cup tomato paste
1 tbsp. lemon juice

salt
pepper
garlic powder
crackers

Place large whole eggplant in microwave and cook at 50 percent power for about 12 minutes or until eggplant is soft. Remove from microwave oven and let cool.

Peel eggplant and chop finely. Measure olive oil and onion into a large bowl; cook at 50 percent power for 3 minutes. Add chopped eggplant and tomato paste. Cook for additional 4 minutes. Add lemon juice and stir well to mix thoroughly. Season with salt, pepper, and garlic powder to taste. Chill and serve with crackers. Makes about two cups.

LOUIE'S CANAPES

½ lb. flaked white fish
½ tsp. prepared mustard
1 tsp. Worcestershire sauce
2 tsp. white horseradish

½ cup mayonnaise
½ tsp. lemon juice
dash of Accent
about 20 crackers

Combine all ingredients except crackers. Place 2 level measuring teaspoons of mixture on each cracker. Place about 8 crackers on microwave-safe plate. Set microwave control at "Defrost." Cook 1 to 1½ minutes. Set control at "Keep Warm." Cook 2 minutes to 2 minutes 15 seconds longer. Repeat for remaining canapes. Makes twenty canapes.

LOVER'S LOX

1 8-oz. pkg. softened cream
  cheese
1 tbsp. mayonnaise
dash lime juice
dash garlic powder
1 large shallot, white part
  only, minced

½ cup diced lox
½ tsp. Worcestershire
  sauce
dash hot pepper sauce

Mix all ingredients together and chill. Serve with crackers or rye rounds. Makes ½ pint.

MON CHER'S MOLD

10 oz. canned tuna fish,
   drained
1 cup softened butter, cut
   into 1-inch pieces
¼ tsp. lemon juice
2 to 3 drops Tabasco sauce
salt and pepper to taste

1 slice lox (about ⅛ lb.)
3 tbsp. coarsely chopped
   pimentos
2 tbsp. capers, drained
parsley sprigs
buttered toast rounds

In food processor with metal blade, place tuna, butter, lemon juice, Tabasco sauce, salt, and pepper. Process until the mixture is smooth. Add lox, pimentos, and capers. Process, turning on and off rapidly, until ingredients are evenly chopped and combined. Taste and adjust seasoning. Mixture should be highly seasoned. Add additional drop of Tabasco if necessary.

Grease a 3-cup loaf pan or mold and pack with paté. Chill for 24 hours. Unmold onto a serving plate. Garnish with parsley and serve with toast rounds. Makes about three cups.

PIERRE'S PATÉ

1 15½ oz. can salmon,
   drained
1 8-oz. pkg. cream cheese,
   softened
2 tbsp. chopped shallots,
   with tops
1 tbsp. lemon juice

½ tsp. salt
⅛ tsp. pepper
2 tbsp. coarsely chopped
   pimento-stuffed olives
assorted crackers or melba
   toast

In food processor with metal blade, process salmon, cream cheese, shallots, lemon juice, salt, and pepper until smooth. Spoon mixture into small bowl. Stir in chopped stuffed olives.

Cover bowl and refrigerate until well chilled. Serve with crackers or melba toast. Makes about 2½ cups.

ST. MARTINVILLE
SALMON SPREAD

1 8-oz. pkg. cream cheese,
  softened
3 tbsp. sherry
1 tsp. Worcestershire sauce
1 tsp. lemon juice
1/8 tsp. Tabasco sauce

salt to taste
1 6½-oz. can salmon,
  drained
¼ cup coarsely chopped
  pecans
crackers or toast rounds

MICROWAVE: In a 3-cup glass bowl or microwave-safe serving dish, stir cream cheese until smooth. Add sherry, Worcestershire sauce, lemon juice, Tabasco sauce, and salt. Stir well. Pick over salmon, discarding any pieces of cartilage, bone, or skin. Stir into cream cheese mixture. Cover tightly with plastic wrap, turning back edge to vent. Microwave at 50 percent power for 5 minutes until hot and bubbly. Stir a few times while cooking. Season to taste. Sprinkle with chopped pecans. Let stand 3 minutes, then serve with crackers or toast rounds. Serves eight to ten.

CONVENTIONAL: Preheat oven to 350° F. Prepare cream cheese and salmon mixture as for microwave method. Spoon mixture into a small baking dish and bake for 15 to 20 minutes or until hot and bubbly. Sprinkle with chopped pecans and serve with crackers or toast rounds. Serves eight to ten.

BECKY'S BLACK-EYED PEA SALAD

2 small apples, peeled and
  cored
¼ cup sweet relish
2 ribs celery
¼ small bell pepper

1 small onion
1 15-oz. can black-eyed
  peas, drained
Becky's Salad Dressing (see
  recipe)

In food processor fitted with steel knife, place apples, relish, celery, bell pepper, and onion. Pulse 2 or 3 times until coarsely chopped. Do not overprocess. Mix with drained peas. Add the dressing. Store covered in the refrigerator for several hours to allow flavors to blend before serving. Serves six to eight.

BECKY'S SALAD DRESSING

½ cup sugar
½ cup water
2 tbsp. flour
⅛ tsp. salt

½ cup white vinegar
2 eggs
½ tsp. dry mustard

Mix all ingredients together. Cook in the top of a double boiler, over simmering water, until thick. Set aside and allow to cool.

CHICKEN SALAD GABRIEL

½ tsp. dry mustard
½ tsp. warm water
⅓ cup salad oil
3 tbsp. lemon juice
½ tsp. celery seeds
salt and pepper to taste
1 clove garlic, minced

2 cups cooked, cubed
  chicken
1 cup diced celery
1 large tart apple, cored
  and sliced
¼ cup chopped pecans

Combine mustard and water and set aside for 10 minutes. Add oil, lemon juice, celery seeds, salt, pepper, and garlic, mixing well. Add chicken, celery, and apple. Toss with dressing. Sprinkle with chopped pecans. Serves four.

CO-CO'S CORN SALAD

4 ears cooked fresh corn
1 large tomato, peeled and
chopped
½ green pepper, cut into
thin strips

3 shallots, thinly sliced
¼ cup chopped parsley
Co-Co's Dressing (see
recipe)

Cut kernels off corn. In a large salad bowl, toss corn, tomato, green pepper, shallots, and parsley. Pour dressing over salad and toss again to coat evenly. Serves four.

CO-CO'S DRESSING

¼ cup salad oil
2 tbsp. tarragon vinegar
1 tsp. lemon juice

½ tsp. salt
1 tsp. prepared mustard
1 tsp. dried basil

Combine all ingredients. Chill. Shake well before using.

DUDLEY'S COLESLAW

2 shallots, white part only,
  cut into 1-inch lengths
1 small head cabbage
  (about 1½ lbs.)
1 medium carrot
½ cup mayonnaise

1 tbsp. white vinegar
2 tsp. prepared mustard
½ tsp. dill seed
½ tsp. sugar
½ tsp. salt
⅛ tsp. pepper

In food processor with metal blade in place, place shallots and pulse until finely minced. Remove and place in large mixing bowl. Change to slicing disc. Remove core from cabbage, cut in half or into sections to fit into feed tube. Stand cabbage sections upright in feed tube and slice, using pulse lever and medium pressure on the feed tube pusher. Remove cabbage and place in large mixing bowl.

Change to shredding disc. Cut carrot into pieces of equal height to fit feed tube. Insert into feed tube and shred, using medium pressure on pusher. Add to cabbage.

Change to metal blade and mix together mayonnaise, vinegar, mustard, dill seed, sugar, salt, and pepper. Add dressing to cabbage mixture and toss to coat evenly. Chill at least 1 hour before serving. Serves four to six.

MALKE'S MACARONI SALAD

2 cups elbow macaroni
1 tbsp. salt
3 qts. boiling water
2 cups diced cooked beets
1 cup thinly sliced raw
  carrots
½ cup thinly sliced
  cucumber

⅓ cup chopped shallots
¼ cup vegetable oil
1 tbsp. vinegar
½ tsp. salt
½ tsp. horseradish

Gradually add macaroni and 1 tablespoon salt to rapidly boiling water. Allow water to continue to boil. Cook uncovered, stirring occasionally, until macaroni is tender. Drain, rinse with cold water, and then drain again thoroughly.

In a large bowl arrange macaroni, beets, carrots, cucumber and shallots. In a small jar combine oil, vinegar, ½ teaspoon salt, and horseradish. Shake well. Pour over macaroni-vegetable mixture. Cover and chill. Toss well before serving. Serves six.

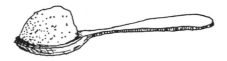

PIROGUE POTATO SALAD

6 medium-size potatoes,
  scrubbed but not peeled
1 cup finely chopped
  shallots
⅔ cup chicken stock
⅓ cup olive oil
1 tbsp. white vinegar

2 tsp. prepared hot mustard
2 tsp. salt
1 tsp. black pepper
1 tbsp. fresh lemon juice
2 drops Tabasco sauce
2 hard-cooked eggs,
  chopped

Drop the unpeeled potatoes into enough lightly salted boiling water to cover them completely. Boil briskly until they can be pierced with the point of a small knife. Do not overcook. Drain potatoes; then peel and cut into ¼-inch slices. Set aside in a tightly covered bowl. Allow to come to room temperature.

In a heavy 2- to 3-quart saucepan, combine chopped shallots, chicken stock, oil, vinegar, mustard, salt, and pepper. Bring to a boil over high heat, stirring occasionally. Reduce heat to low and simmer, uncovered, for 5 minutes. Remove pan from heat and stir in lemon juice and Tabasco.

Add chopped eggs to potato slices; toss gently. Pour sauce over potatoes and egg, turning to coat them evenly. Serve at room temperature or chilled. Serves four.

RENÉ'S RICE SALAD

4½ cups cooked hot rice
¼ cup salad oil
2 tbsp. white vinegar
2 tbsp. prepared mustard
1½ tsp. salt
⅛ tsp. pepper

2 hard-cooked eggs, diced
⅓ cup diced celery
¼ cup chopped pimento
   olives
1 small onion, minced
½ cup René's Mayonnaise
   (see recipe)

Blend together salad oil, vinegar, mustard, salt, and pepper. Pour over hot rice. Toss. Set aside to cool. Add remaining ingredients in the order listed. Toss again and chill thoroughly. Serve on lettuce leaves. Serves four to six.

RENÉ'S MAYONNAISE

1 whole egg
1 tbsp. lemon juice
1 tsp. salt

¼ tsp. freshly ground
   pepper
1½ cups salad oil

In food processor with metal blade in place, place the egg, lemon juice, salt, and pepper. Process until blended, about 2 to 3 seconds. Continue processing while gradually pouring oil through feed tube. Continue to process until mayonnaise thickens. Taste and add lemon juice, salt, and pepper if needed. This mayonnaise will keep for a week in the refrigerator. Makes about 1¾ cups.

SHRIMP?! SALAD

4 cups chilled cooked rice
1 16-oz. can salmon,
  drained and flaked
½ cup chopped celery
3 hard-cooked eggs,
  chopped

½ cup chopped parsley
salt and pepper to taste
Shrimp?! Salad Dressing
  (see recipe)

Toss all ingredients together. Pour dressing over salad. Chill for 3 to 4 hours. Serves six to eight.

SHRIMP?! SALAD DRESSING

2 tbsp. olive oil
2 tbsp. tarragon vinegar

½ cup mayonnaise

Whisk oil, vinegar, and mayonnaise together until well blended.

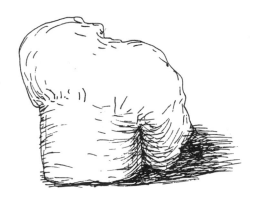

TZADIK'S THREE-BEAN SALAD

1 cup cooked red beans
1 cup cooked green beans
1 cup cooked yellow wax
  beans
¾ cup finely chopped
  shallots
½ tsp. finely chopped
  garlic
2 tbsp. finely chopped
  parsley

1 small green pepper,
  seeded and coarsely
  chopped
1 tsp. salt
freshly ground black pepper
3 tbsp. vinegar
½ cup olive oil

In a large bowl combine red beans, green beans, wax beans, shallots, garlic, parsley, and green pepper. Add salt, a few grindings of pepper, and vinegar. Toss gently with a large spoon. Pour in olive oil and toss again. Chill for 1 hour before serving. Serves six to eight.

ZACK'S ZUCCHINI SALAD

4 medium-size zucchini
1 bunch shallots
1 green pepper
1 stalk celery
¼ tsp. salt

1 medium-size yellow
  squash
⅓ cup sugar
⅓ cup cider vinegar
3 tbsp. salad oil

In food processor with shredding disc in place, shred zucchini and yellow squash. Place shallots, green pepper, and celery in processor fitted with metal blade. Pulse on and off until vegetables are coarsely chopped. Do not overprocess. Put zucchini, squash, shallots, green pepper, and celery into a large salad bowl. Mix salt, sugar, vinegar, and salad oil together until well blended. Pour over vegetable mixture and toss well. Cover and chill for at least 1 hour before serving. Serves six to eight.

New Iberia
SAUCES AND SEASONINGS

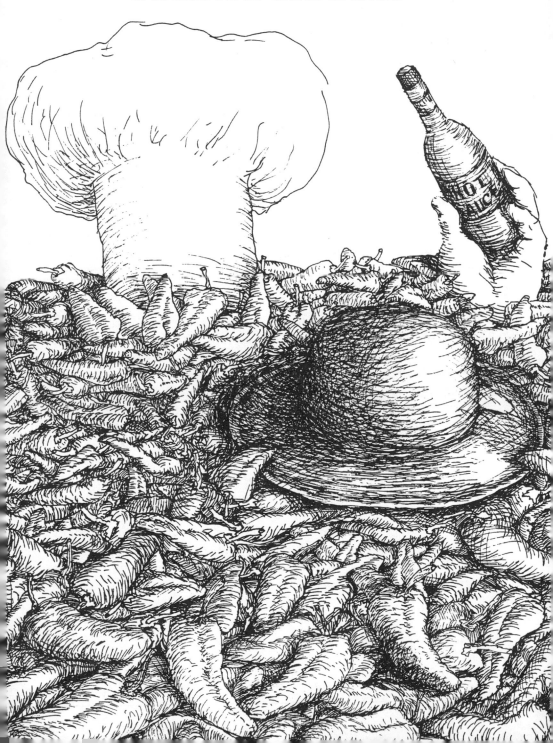

Iberia Parish lies in the heart of Acadiana. It is Cajun country at its best – a fascinating world all its own, an area like no other. Whatever your fancy, Iberia Parish has it for you: There are plantations, gardens, camp grounds, Indian trail rides, and paddlewheel boats on the bayou; salt domes, sulphur deposits, muskrat, and fur trapping; and canneries, rice mills, and condiment factories.

New Iberia, the main town in the parish, is variously called "The Queen City of the Teche" and "The Hottest Town in the United States." The waters and shoreline of Bayou Teche provide a panoramic view of Cajun culture. The eighteenth century old-world setting is preserved in a modern community. The culture has been further preserved by the restoration of the Mintmere Plantation and the Armand Broussard House, each displaying a distinct style of nineteenth century Louisiana architecture.

Beautiful moss-draped oaks and cypress trees line the banks of the bayou. The Jungle Garden, with its exotic tropical gardens and bird sanctuary, is on nearby Avery Island, which is the home of the famous Tabasco sauce. The peppers used in the sauce derive their distinctive and unusual flavor from the island's salt domes on which they are grown.

New Iberia and its few adjoining parishes are the only place in North America where millions of pounds of little peppers, Chili Cortidos, Sports, and other peppers are grown successfully. This crop provides the ingredients for the celebrated hot sauces that are shipped all over the nation. From these "little red devils" a major Southern industry thrives today, and the modern factories and mills producing these condiments have made New Iberia the "hot spot" of the nation.

The story of this industry begins in 1848, when Col. Maunsell White, a well-known Southern planter, was given some red pepper seeds by a Mexican friend. A few summers later, the colonel found acres of his land flourishing with bushes laden with red, green, and yellow peppers. So pleased was he with this extraordinary crop, which he discovered possessed an extremely fine flavor, that he named them after the Mexican state from which they had come, Tabasco. By 1898, B. F. Trappey, originally a blacksmith, turned to farming and became interested in the Tabasco pepper. In huge pepper vats, he experimented with various processings and blendings until he developed his renowned hot pepper sauces and products.

Today, the modern manufacturing plants, paradoxically rising above placid Bayou Teche, supply Cajun cooks with the seasonings for their unique cooking. It is these delicious herbs and spices that produce the distinctive flavor of Cajun cooking. To the people of this area, this is the true meaning of the phrase, "the spice of life."

SAUCES AND SEASONINGS

Avery Island Herb Butter *(Processor)*
Bayou Teche Barbecue Sauce *(Microwave)*
Blanc Sauce *(Conventional)*
The Colonel's Remoulade Sauce *(Processor)*
Everyone's Basic Roux *(Conventional)*
Hollandaise Sauce *(Microwave and Conventional)*
Honey Pecan Sauce *(Processor)*
Jungle Sauce Piquante *(Conventional)*
Kosher Cajun Seasoning Mix I *(Conventional)*
Kosher Cajun Seasoning Mix II *(Conventional)*
Kosher Cajun Seasoning Mix III *(Conventional)*
Mintmere Mayonnaise *(Processor)*
New Iberia Garlic Sauce *(Conventional)*
Nippy Fruit Sauce *(Conventional)*
Processor Hollandaise Sauce *(Processor)*
Red Devil Barbeque Sauce *(Conventional)*
Sauce Royale *(Conventional)*
Seasoned Roux *(Microwave)*
Spirited Horseradish Sauce *(Conventional)*
Trappers' Tartar Sauce *(Conventional)*
Vise-ah Sauce *(Microwave)*

AVERY ISLAND HERB BUTTER

½ red bell pepper, cut into
small pieces
2 shallots, chopped
4 cloves garlic, chopped
½ tsp. thyme

1 tbsp. chopped parsley
⅛ tsp. cayenne pepper
1 stick unsalted butter, cut
into pieces

Combine the bell pepper, shallots, garlic, thyme, parsley, and cayenne pepper in a food processor. Pulse on and off until ingredients are minced but not puréed. Add the butter pieces and process until blended. Remove butter to a sheet of plastic wrap and roll into a cylinder about 1½ inches in diameter. Wrap securely in plastic wrap. Freeze until firm (1 to 2 hours). Makes about ten tablespoons butter (ten pats).

BAYOU TECHE BARBECUE SAUCE

2 cups ketchup
1 tbsp. horseradish
½ cup brown sugar
½ cup vinegar
1 tbsp. Worcestershire
sauce

½ tsp. garlic powder
2 medium onions, sliced
½ tsp. salt
⅛ tsp. cayenne pepper
½ cup water

Combine all ingredients in a 2-quart microwave-safe casserole. Cook at 50 percent power for 5 minutes or until onion is tender. Makes three cups.

BLANC SAUCE

¼ cup butter
¼ cup all-purpose flour

1 cup milk, scalded
salt and pepper to taste

Melt butter in a heavy saucepan; blend in flour on low heat, stirring constantly until smooth. Remove from heat; stir in heated milk a little at a time, stirring constantly. Season to taste. Cook on low heat, stirring constantly, until thick and bubbly. Makes one cup.

THE COLONEL'S REMOULADE SAUCE

1¼ cups olive oil
½ cup vinegar
¾ cup Dijon mustard
½ cup ketchup
5 tbsp. prepared
  horseradish

5 cloves garlic, chopped
1 tsp. Tabasco sauce
½ tsp. salt

In a food processor, combine all ingredients. Pulse on and off until well blended. Makes 3 cups.

EVERYONE'S BASIC ROUX

1 cup all-purpose flour

1 cup vegetable oil

Heat oil in a heavy skillet until hot but not smoking. Gradually add flour, stirring constantly until well mixed. Lower flame and continue stirring until roux is caramel in color. Remove from skillet and set aside or refrigerate until ready for use.

HOLLANDAISE SAUCE

½ cup butter
3 egg yolks
2 tbsp. lemon juice

⅛ tsp. salt
dash Tabasco sauce

MICROWAVE: Place butter in a 1-cup glass measure. Microwave at 100 percent power for 1 minute or until melted but not hot. Combine egg yolks, lemon juice, salt, and Tabasco sauce in a glass bowl and stir until smooth. Stir in butter slowly. Microwave at 50 percent power 1½ to 2 minutes, stirring every 30 seconds during the first minute and every 15 seconds during the second minute. Finished sauce should be thick and smooth. Makes about ¾ cup.

CONVENTIONAL: Cut butter into 6 pieces. Beat egg yolks, lemon juice, salt, and Tabasco sauce in the top of a double boiler. Place over barely simmering water. Add 1 piece of butter and cook, stirring constantly, until butter melts. Repeat with remaining pieces of butter. Continue cooking, stirring constantly, until sauce is slightly thickened and smooth. Makes about ¾ cup.

NOTE: If sauce begins to separate, remove from heat immediately, add 1 or 2 tablespoons ice water, and beat rapidly with whisk until smooth again. To keep sauce warm, set container of sauce over warm water, press plastic wrap directly on surface of sauce, and let stand until ready to serve. To reheat sauce in microwave, microwave at 30 percent power for 1½ to 2 minutes, stirring briskly with whisk every 30 seconds.

HONEY PECAN SAUCE

¼ lb. pareve margarine, at
   room temperature

1 cup pecan halves
4 tbsp. honey

Combine all ingredients in the bowl of a food processor fitted with steel blade. Pulse on and off several times to blend ingredients, leaving pecans chunky. Remove from bowl and serve in small crock. Makes 1¼ cups.

JUNGLE SAUCE PIQUANTE

2 cups chopped onions
½ cup vegetable oil
1 cup chopped celery
2 cloves garlic, minced
1 bell pepper, chopped
1 6-oz. can tomato paste
1 8-oz. can tomato sauce

juice and rind of 1 lemon
1 tsp. salt
¼ tsp. cayenne pepper
1 cup fish or chicken stock
¼ cup shallots, chopped
¼ cup chopped parsley

Sauté onions in oil until transparent. Add celery, garlic, bell pepper, tomato paste, tomato sauce, lemon rind, salt, and cayenne pepper. Cook for 45 minutes on low heat. Add stock and stir well. Add lemon juice, shallots, and parsley. Simmer for 5 minutes. Makes 3½ to 4 cups.

KOSHER CAJUN SEASONING
MIX I

½ tsp. salt
½ tsp. freshly ground white
  pepper
¼ tsp. garlic powder
½ tsp. onion powder
½ tsp. cayenne pepper

½ tsp. Hungarian paprika
½ tsp. dried thyme,
  crumbled
¼ tsp. freshly ground black
  pepper

Mix all ingredients. Store in an airtight jar. Makes one heaping tablespoon.

KOSHER CAJUN SEASONING
MIX II

½ tsp. garlic powder
½ tsp. ground white pepper
½ tsp. cayenne pepper

½ tsp. black pepper
¼ tsp. dry mustard
¼ tsp. crushed basil

Mix all ingredients. Store in a covered jar. Makes 2½ teaspoons.

KOSHER CAJUN SEASONING
MIX III

¼ tsp. salt
½ tsp. black pepper
½ tsp. garlic powder
¼ tsp. Accent

¼ tsp. chili powder
⅛ tsp. cayenne pepper
⅛ tsp. thyme

Mix all ingredients. Store in a jar. Makes two teaspoons.

MINTMERE MAYONNAISE

1 egg
1 tbsp. lemon juice
1 tsp. salt

¼ tsp. black or white
    pepper
1½ cups salad oil

In a food processor with metal blade in place, place egg, lemon juice, salt, and pepper. Process until blended. Continue processing while gradually pouring oil through feed tube. Mayonnaise will thicken as oil is added. Adjust seasoning if necessary. Transfer to covered container and refrigerate. Makes about 1¾ cups.

NEW IBERIA GARLIC SAUCE

½ cup melted butter
5 tbsp. fresh lemon juice
3 cloves garlic, minced

⅛ tsp. salt
⅛ tsp. black pepper
dash Tabasco sauce

Combine all ingredients. Blend well. Makes ½ cup.

NIPPY FRUIT SAUCE

1 12-oz. jar pineapple
  preserves
¼ cup prepared mustard

¼ cup prepared
  horseradish

Mix all ingredients together in saucepan. Heat and serve. Makes 1¾ cups.

PROCESSOR HOLLANDAISE
SAUCE

4 egg yolks
2 tbsp. lemon juice
½ tsp. salt
dash Tabasco sauce

½ cup melted unsalted
  butter or pareve
  margarine

In food processor fitted with metal blade, place egg yolks, lemon juice, salt, and Tabasco. Process for 3 seconds. Still processing, slowly pour in hot melted butter or pareve margarine through the feed tube. Process until sauce thickens to consistency of mayonnaise. Be sure butter or margarine is bubbling hot or sauce will not thicken. Makes ¾ cup.

RED DEVIL BARBEQUE SAUCE

2 sticks pareve margarine
¾ cup chopped onion
½ cup brown sugar
¼ tsp. cayenne pepper
1 cup vegetable oil
1 tsp. dry mustard
½ cup Worcestershire
  sauce

1 14-oz. bottle ketchup
2 tbsp. chili sauce
2 cloves garlic, minced
¼ cup lemon juice
3 to 4 drops Tabasco sauce

Melt margarine in a large saucepan. Add onion and sauté until transparent. Add remaining ingredients, stirring constantly. Simmer for about 15 minutes, stirring frequently. Makes 3½ cups.

SAUCE ROYALE

1 cup ketchup
½ tsp. dry mustard
1 tbsp. brown sugar

2 tbsp. vinegar
6 tbsp. pareve margarine

In a saucepan, combine all ingredients. Mix well and cook over medium heat for 4 to 5 minutes, stirring constantly. Serves six.

SEASONED ROUX

½ cup vegetable oil
½ cup all-purpose flour
1 cup chopped onion
½ cup chopped celery
⅓ cup chopped green
   pepper

2 tbsp. minced parsley
2 cloves garlic, minced
hot water

In microwave, melt vegetable oil in a 1-quart glass measure on 100 percent power for 45 seconds. Stir in flour. Microwave on 100 percent power for 7 to 8 minutes or until roux is caramel brown, stirring every minute.

Spoon onion, celery, green pepper, parsley, and garlic on top of roux. Microwave on 100 percent power for 4 minutes or until vegetables are barely tender. Stir into roux. Slowly stir in enough hot tap water to make 3 cups roux. Makes 3 cups.

SPIRITED HORSERADISH SAUCE

1 tsp. prepared mustard
2 tbsp. prepared
   horseradish
1 tbsp. tarragon vinegar
1 tsp. chopped onion

¼ tsp. Tabasco sauce
¼ tsp. salt
¼ tsp. black pepper
1 cup ketchup

Combine mustard and horseradish. Blend in vinegar until smooth. Add onion, Tabasco, salt, pepper, and ketchup. Mix well. Makes 1 cup.

TRAPPERS' TARTAR SAUCE

1 cup mayonnaise
½ tsp. dry mustard
4 tsp. finely chopped
 shallots
1 tbsp. chopped sweet
 pickle, drained
1 clove garlic, minced

1 tsp. tarragon vinegar
⅛ tsp. salt
⅛ tsp. black pepper
⅛ tsp. cayenne pepper

Mix all ingredients until well blended. Store in refrigerator until ready to use. Makes 1¼ cups.

VISE-AH SAUCE

2 tbsp. butter
2 tbsp. flour

½ tsp. salt
1 cup milk

In microwave melt butter in a 1-quart microwave-safe casserole for 30 seconds on 50 percent power. Stir in flour and salt and blend to a smooth paste. Add milk gradually, stirring constantly. Cook, uncovered, on 50 percent power for 1 minute. Stir well. Cook 1½ to 2 minutes longer at 50 percent power, stirring after every 30 seconds. Makes 1 cup.

Morgan City
SEAFOOD

Morgan City, the "Queen City" on the Atchafalaya River, is an island seaport famous not only for having the world's first offshore oil well but also as a colorful fishing and hunting center, nicknamed "Tiger Island." It is often referred to as a sportsman's paradise.

Perhaps the outstanding attraction in Morgan City is the living museum. Here one becomes aware of the story of the Great Swamp and the adventurous struggle for survival of its earlier settlers. The Original Swamp Gardens are in a preserved area of swampland. They depict the life of Cajun pioneers and, in earlier days, the Indians. The Gardens are a tribute designed to recall the heritage of the Great Swamp and the courage and determination of those people who played such an important part in developing South Louisiana.

Mother Nature has graced this last great river wilderness area in America with a spectacular show. Traveling through the Great Swamp is unforgettable. The ancient bayou winds its way past bald cypress trees (the state tree) draped with gray Spanish moss. From the marshes dart the nutria, muskrats, minks, otters, and other small fur-bearing animals. The alligators that bask so peacefully along the banks spring to life all too suddenly and head toward the pirogues paddling by. Then, like all good things that must come to an end, the bayou slowly dissolves into the backwater, a remote area which is part of the Delta Flood Plain.

Morgan City is friendly and charming, best known for its fishing vessels, its delicious seafood, and its festivals. The excitement begins with the oldest chartered harvest festival in Louisiana, the Shrimp and Petroleum Festival held on Labor Day weekend. This celebration honors the seafood and oil industries, which are the main source of the area's economy. There are parades, Cajun music, boat races, and the crowning of the festival king and queen. But the highlight of the festival is the ecumenical blessing of the brightly decorated shrimp fleet. Following the blessing, the shrimping season officially opens, and the festivities begin.

In addition to its natural beauty and its history, Morgan City offers the tourist the chance to discover the joys of Cajun family life along the bayou and the traditions that have kept these down-home folks close to the land of their ancestors. They still "parlons français ici" (speak French here) and indisputably proclaim their distinctive Cajun homestyle cooking "la bonne cuisine" (the good cooking).

SEAFOOD

Backwater Baked Fish *(Microwave)*
Cantor's Courtbouillon *(Microwave and Processor)*
Curled-up Flounder *(Microwave and Conventional)*
Feisty Fish Stew *(Conventional)*
Flounder-ing Lox *(Processor and Conventional)*
Fried Katz Fish *(Conventional)*
Kosher Krab Kakes *(Processor and Conventional)*
Morgan City Fish Stock *(Conventional)*
Oy!-Sters Bennyville *(Conventional)*
Queen City Casserole *(Microwave and Conventional)*
Redfish from the Parish *(Microwave)*
Scalloped Gefilte Fish *(Conventional)*
Schvarzadick Redfish *(Conventional)*
Sea-gel's Strudel *(Conventional)*
Seaport Kabobs *(Microwave)*
Snapper Noir *(Processor and Conventional)*
Stuffed Krabettes *(Processor and Conventional)*
Tiger Island Tuna *(Processor and Conventional)*
Trayfish Beignets *(Processor and Conventional)*
Tripp's Tuna Wedges *(Microwave)*
Trout Filled to the Gills *(Microwave and Processor)*
Veggie-Lox Pasta *(Conventional)*

BACKWATER BAKED FISH

1 whole fish (about 1 lb.),
  gutted and cleaned
4 tbsp. butter or margarine,
  melted
½ tsp. salt

¼ tsp. black pepper
¼ tsp. paprika
2 tbsp. grated onion
2 cups bread cubes
¾ tsp. chopped chives

Brush inside of fish with some of the melted butter or margarine and sprinkle with salt, pepper, and paprika. Place 2 tablespoons melted butter and the onion in an 8-inch round glass dish. Cook in microwave on 50 percent power (Medium) for about 2 minutes or until onion is transparent. Add bread cubes. Stir. Fill cavity of fish and lace closed with string and round wooden toothpicks.

Place fish in a 1½-quart oblong dish. Brush fish well with remaining melted butter. Sprinkle with chopped chives. Cover. Cook 11 to 13 minutes or until fish flakes easily with a fork. Serves two.

CANTOR'S COURTBOUILLON

6 to 8 lbs. redfish or red
  snapper, cut into pieces
1 cup flour
1 cup butter
2 large onions, chopped
6 stalks celery, chopped
  (about 1 cup)
1 bell pepper, chopped
2 cloves garlic, chopped
1 8-oz. can tomato sauce
1 6-oz. can tomate paste
1 qt. water

1 tbsp. Worcestershire
  sauce
½ lemon, sliced
½ tsp. garlic salt
½ tsp. ground white pepper
½ tsp. cayenne pepper
½ tsp. black pepper
¼ tsp. dry mustard
¼ tsp. crushed basil
¼ cup chopped shallot tops
¼ cup chopped parsley

Place butter in a 2-quart bowl. Microwave on 70 percent power (Medium-High) for 1 to 2 minutes or until butter is melted. Add flour and stir. Microwave on High for 8 to 9 minutes or until roux is a rich dark brown, stirring when there are 4 minutes, 2 minutes, 1 minute, and 30 seconds left on the timer.

In food processor fitted with steel blade, process onions, celery, bell pepper, and garlic until chopped fine.

In a 5-quart casserole, combine roux, chopped vegetables, tomato sauce, tomato paste, water, Worcestershire sauce, and lemon. Cover with plastic wrap. Microwave on High for 10 minutes, then on 50 percent power for 20 minutes.

In a small bowl, mix garlic salt, white pepper, cayenne pepper, black pepper, dry mustard, and basil. Sprinkle seasonings over fish. Add fish to mixture. Cover with plastic wrap.

Microwave on 50 percent power for 15 to 20 minutes or until fish is done. Let stand 5 minutes before serving. Top with shallot tops and parsley. Serves eight.

CURLED-UP FLOUNDER

1 medium-size onion, chopped
1 cup sliced mushrooms
3 tbsp. butter or margarine
1/2 tsp. fines herbes
1/2 tsp. salt
1/4 tsp. black pepper
1 cup bread cubes

2 tbsp. dry white wine (plus additional 1/2 cup for conventional method)
6 flounder fillets (about 2 lbs.)
Hollandaise Sauce (see recipe)

MICROWAVE: Butter six 6-ounce custard cups. Combine onion, mushrooms, and butter in a glass mixing bowl. Cover tightly with plastic wrap, turning back edge to vent. Microwave at 100 percent power for 3 minutes. Stir in seasonings, bread cubes, and 2 tablespoons wine. Spoon a little stuffing onto the darker side of each fillet. Roll up, starting at narrow end, to form a turban. Place one turban in each cup. Cover each cup tightly with plastic wrap, turning back edges to vent. Place cups in a circle in microwave oven. Microwave at 70 percent power for 12 to 14 minutes or until fish flakes easily, rotating cups once. Let stand 3 minutes. Invert turbans from cups and serve with Hollandaise Sauce. Serves six.

CONVENTIONAL: Butter a 10-inch × 6-inch baking dish. Preheat oven to 350° F. Sauté onion and mushrooms in butter until onion is transparent. Stir in seasonings, bread cubes, and 2 tablespoons wine. Spoon a little stuffing onto darker side of each fillet. Roll up, starting at narrow end. Place in prepared baking dish. Pour ½ cup wine around turbans and bake about 25 minutes or until fish flakes easily. Serve with Hollandaise Sauce. Serves six.

FEISTY FISH STEW

2 lbs. fresh fish fillets
⅓ cup all-purpose flour
⅓ cup vegetable oil
2½ cups fish stock
2 large onions, sliced and separated into rings
2 large red or green sweet peppers, coarsely chopped
3 banana peppers, seeded and sliced crosswise

2 cloves garlic, minced
½ tsp. salt
½ tsp. ground cayenne pepper
¼ tsp. black pepper
¼ tsp. Tabasco sauce
2 sweet potatoes (about 1 lb.), peeled and sliced
1 tsp. filé powder
hot cooked rice (optional)

In a heavy 4-quart saucepan or Dutch oven, stir together the flour and vegetable oil until smooth. Cook over medium-high heat for 5 minutes, stirring constantly. Reduce heat to medium. Cook and stir constantly for 15 to 20 minutes or until a reddish-brown roux is formed.

Gradually stir fish stock into roux. Stir in onions, peppers, garlic, salt, cayenne pepper, black pepper, and Tabasco sauce. Bring to a boil, reduce heat, cover, and simmer for 10 minutes. Add sweet potatoes; simmer, covered, 10 minutes more. Add fish. Simmer, covered, about 5 minutes or until fish flakes easily when tested with a fork. Remove from heat. Stir in filé powder. Serve over hot cooked rice, if desired. Serves six.

FLOUNDER-ING LOX

3 stalks celery, finely
  chopped
3 shallots with tops, finely
  chopped
1 clove garlic, finely
  chopped
¼ lb. plus 1 tbsp. butter
1½ cups moistened
  seasoned bread crumbs

½ lb. lox, coarsely chopped
½ lb. smoked trout, boned
  and flaked
2 tbsp. chopped parsley
1 egg, slightly beaten
¼ tsp. salt
¼ tsp. black pepper
⅛ tsp. cayenne pepper
4 flounders

In food processor fitted with metal blade, process celery, shallots, and garlic until finely chopped. In a large skillet, melt 4 tablespoons butter over low heat. Sauté vegetables until soft and limp. Add bread crumbs, chopped lox, flaked fish, parsley, and egg to vegetables and mix well. Season with salt, black pepper, and cayenne and remove from heat.

Split thick side of flounder lengthwise and crosswise and loosen meat from bones of fish to form a pocket for stuffing. Brush pocket with 1 tablespoon melted butter and stuff with lox mixture. Melt remaining 4 tablespoons of butter in a shallow baking pan large enough to hold the fish without overlapping. Arrange fish in pan. Cover and bake at 375° F. for 25 minutes or until fish flakes easily with a fork. Remove cover and bake an additional 5 minutes. Serves four.

FRIED KATZ FISH

vegetable oil for deep frying
1 egg
½ cup milk
½ tsp. salt
¼ tsp. pepper
¼ tsp. paprika
¼ cup yellow cornmeal

6 fish fillets (about 3 lbs.),
such as trout, redfish,
sole or 6 whole small
fish, such as perch,
croaker
lemon wedges (optional)

In a deep skillet, heat oil to 350° F. (deep-frying temperature). Beat egg and milk together; set aside. Combine salt, pepper, paprika, and cornmeal. Dip fish fillets in egg mixture and then in cornmeal mixture, coating both sides evenly. Deep-fry fish until golden brown on both sides and fish flakes easily with fork. Drain on absorbent paper and serve with lemon wedges, if desired. Serves six.

KOSHER KRAB KAKES

1 lb. smoked white fish,
skinned, boned, and
flaked
1 cup mayonnaise
3 tbsp. flour
½ bell pepper, finely
chopped
1 small onion, finely
chopped

1 stalk celery, finely
chopped
½ cup matzo meal
⅛ tsp. cayenne pepper
¼ tsp. minced parsley
vegetable oil for frying

In food processor fitted with metal blade, process bell pepper, onion, and celery until finely chopped. Combine flaked fish, mayonnaise, flour, and chopped vegetables. Form into patties. Mix matzo meal with cayenne pepper and minced parsley. Coat each patty with matzo meal mixture.

Pour enough oil into a large pan to cover the bottom. Over medium heat, fry patties until brown, turning once. Drain on absorbent paper. Serves four to six.

MORGAN CITY FISH STOCK

5 to 6 lbs. fish heads,
  bones, and scraps
1 leek, washed and split
2 shallots, with tops, cut in
  half
1 medium onion, quartered
4 cloves garlic, cut in half
2 bay leaves

1 large carrot, quartered
2 medium stalks celery,
  each cut into 4 pieces
½ tsp. dill weed
¼ tsp. salt
4 white peppercorns
1 cup dry white wine

Rinse the fish scraps well and drain. Put into a large kettle and cover with water. Bring to a boil, skimming the foam as it comes to the top. Simmer for 15 minutes, continuing to skim. Add the remaining ingredients and simmer for 1 hour.

Strain through a triple layer of cheesecloth and let cool, uncovered. Remove any fat and scum. Return to heat and continue to simmer until liquid is reduced to about 2½ quarts. Store in refrigerator or freezer.

OY!-STERS BENNYVILLE

1 bunch shallots, with tops,
  chopped
3 tbsp. butter
3 tbsp. flour
¾ cup milk
¼ cup kosher white wine

1 2-oz. can mushrooms
2 tbsp. seasoned bread
  crumbs
2 tbsp. grated Parmesan
  cheese
4 large gefilte fish pieces

Cook shallots in butter until tender but not brown. Add flour, milk, and wine. Cook until thick, about 15 minutes, on medium heat. Add mushrooms and cook for about 2 more minutes.

Slice gefilte fish pieces into ½-inch slices. Line the bottom of a 1½-quart rectangular casserole dish with slices of gefilte fish. Pour sauce over fish. Sprinkle with bread crumbs mixed with cheese. Bake in a 400-degree oven for about 10 minutes or until cheese is brown. Serves four.

QUEEN CITY CASSEROLE

1 onion, sliced
1 tbsp. lemon juice
2 sprigs parsley
1 bay leaf

salt and pepper to taste
water
1 lb. fish fillets

SAUCE:

1 egg, lightly beaten
2 tbsp. mayonnaise
1 tbsp. dry sherry
2 tbsp. dry mustard
salt and pepper to taste

⅛ tsp. Tabasco sauce
1 green pepper, diced
2 tbsp. diced pimento
2 tbsp. chopped parsley
¼ tsp. paprika

MICROWAVE: Place onion, lemon juice, parsley, bay leaf, salt, pepper, and ½ cup water in a 10-by-6-inch glass baking dish. Cover tightly with plastic wrap, turning back edge to vent. Microwave at 100 percent power for 4 minutes. Add fish. Cover, leaving vent, and microwave at 100 percent power for 5 minutes or until fish flakes easily. Let stand, covered, for 3 minutes. Lift fish from cooking liquid with slotted spatula. Drain fish well and break into large flakes. Set aside.

Lightly grease a 1-quart casserole. Combine egg, mayonnaise, sherry, mustard, salt, pepper, and Tabasco sauce in a medium-size bowl. Stir in green pepper, pimento, and parsley. Gently fold in flaked fish and spoon into prepared casserole. Sprinkle lightly with paprika. Cover tightly with plastic wrap, turning back edge to vent. Microwave at 70 percent power 5 minutes or until hot, rotating casserole once. Let stand, covered, for 3 minutes. Serves four.

CONVENTIONAL: Place onion, lemon juice, parsley, bay leaf, salt, pepper, and 1 cup water in a 10-inch skillet. Heat to boiling. Reduce heat, cover, and simmer for 10 minutes. Add fish, cover, and simmer for 5 minutes or until fish flakes easily. Remove from cooking liquid with slotted spatula. Drain fish well and break into large flakes. Set aside.

Preheat oven to 375° F. Lightly grease a 1-quart casserole. Combine egg, mayonnaise, sherry, mustard, salt, pepper, and Tabasco sauce in a medium-size bowl. Stir in green pepper, pimento, and parsley. Gently fold in flaked fish and spoon into prepared casserole. Sprinkle lightly with paprika. Bake 15 minutes or until heated through and top begins to brown. Serves four.

REDFISH FROM THE PARISH

2 tbsp. olive oil
½ cup chopped onion
2 tsp. minced garlic
1 16-oz. can tomatoes, crushed
⅓ cup dry white wine
2 tbsp. chopped fresh basil
1 tsp. chopped fresh thyme
1 bay leaf
½ tsp. salt
½ tsp. sugar
⅛ tsp. cayenne pepper
1 tbsp. butter
1 lb. redfish or red snapper fillets

In a shallow, 1-quart microwaveproof dish, microwave olive oil on High for 2 minutes. Add onion and garlic; microwave on High for 5 minutes, stirring once. Stir in crushed tomatoes, wine, basil, thyme, bay leaf, salt, sugar, and cayenne pepper. Microwave on High for 12 minutes, stirring occasionally. Stir in butter.

Cut fish into 4 pieces and arrange in dish. Spoon sauce over fish. Microwave on Medium for 6 minutes, rearranging fish after 3 minutes. Microwave on High for 13 minutes; halfway through cooking, rearrange fish, stir sauce, and rotate dish. Let stand 3 minutes. Discard bay leaf before serving. Serves four.

SCALLOPED GEFILTE FISH

1 16-oz. jar (4 pieces)
  gefilte fish in liquid broth
¼ cup tarragon vinegar
¼ cup minced shallots
½ cup bread crumbs
1 clove garlic, minced
¼ tsp. dill weed
¼ tsp. lemon zest

¼ tsp. thyme
2 tsp. butter
½ cup heavy cream, at
  room temperature
⅛ tsp. Herbsaint liqueur
¼ cup grated Parmesan
  cheese

Preheat the oven to 375° F. Drain gefilte fish and reserve liquid. Slice each piece of fish vertically, into 3 pieces (total of 12 pieces). Put fish pieces into a bowl and toss with the vinegar. Drain again. Toss the shallots with the bread crumbs, garlic, dill, lemon zest, and thyme.

Butter an ovenproof dish and coat lightly with seasoned bread crumbs. Add the drained fish pieces, reserved liquid, cream, and Herbsaint. Top with the remaining bread crumbs and the cheese and dot with the remaining butter. Bake for 5 to 6 minutes or until the sauce is bubbling and the crumbs are lightly browned. Serves four.

SCHVARZADICK REDFISH

4 redfish fillets (8 to 10 oz.
  each)
½ tsp. salt
1 medium onion, thinly
  sliced
4 large cloves garlic,
  coarsely chopped

1½ tsp. black pepper
1 tsp. thyme
½ tsp. oregano
¼ tsp. cayenne pepper
1 cup butter, melted
2 lemons, cut into wedges
  (optional)

In a shallow dish, season fish with salt and top with onion and garlic. Cover tightly and refrigerate for 3 to 4 hours.

In a small bowl combine black pepper, thyme, oregano, and cayenne pepper. Scrape onion and garlic from fish. Brush fish on both sides with some butter. Sprinkle evenly with pepper mixture.

Heat a cast-iron skillet over high heat. Add half the fish, skin side down, and cook for 3 minutes or until completely charred, drizzling more butter on top. Turn and cook for 2 minutes more. Transfer to platter; keep warm. Discard butter drippings and wipe out skillet. Repeat with remaining fish and butter. Serve with lemon wedges, if desired. Serves four to six.

NOTE: This recipe creates a great deal of smoke. Make sure your kitchen is well ventilated and use exhaust fans if possible.

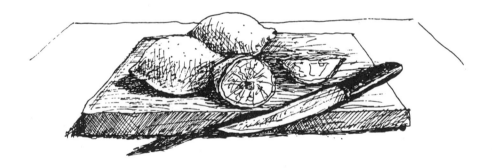

SEA-GEL'S STRUDEL

10 tbsp. butter or
   margarine
1 tbsp. finely chopped
   shallots
3 tbsp. all-purpose flour
1/4 tsp. salt
1/8 tsp. black pepper
1 1/3 cups milk

1 lb. smoked fish
   (whitefish, smoked trout,
   smoked carp), boned and
   flaked
3 tbsp. dry sherry
1/3 16-oz. pkg. frozen phyllo
   dough
1/4 cup bread crumbs

In a 2-quart saucepan, melt 4 tablespoons butter. Sauté chopped shallots until tender, stirring occasionally. Stir in flour, salt, and pepper and cook for 1 minute. Gradually stir milk into flour mixture, stirring constantly until mixture thickens and is smooth. Stir in fish and sherry. Remove saucepan from heat and set aside.

In a small saucepan over low heat, melt 4 tablespoons butter. On waxed paper or a damp kitchen towel, overlap a few sheets of phyllo dough to make a 16-inch × 12-inch rectangle. Brush each sheet of phyllo with some of the remaining melted butter. Sprinkle with 1 tablespoon bread crumbs. Continue layering, brushing each sheet of phyllo with some butter and sprinkling every other layer with 1 tablespoon bread crumbs.

Preheat oven to 375° F. Starting along a short side of phyllo, evenly spoon fish mixture to cover about half of rectangle. Starting on the mixture side, roll phyllo, jelly-roll fashion. Place roll seam side down on cookie sheet. Brush with butter. Bake for 40 minutes or until golden. Cool strudel about 15 minutes before slicing into 1-inch pieces. Makes 12 pieces.

SEAPORT KABOBS

20 small (cocktail-size)
gefilte fish balls
1 4-oz. can button
mushrooms, drained
3 tbsp. salad oil
1 tbsp. Worcestershire
sauce
3 tbsp. lemon juice
2 tsp. parsley flakes

¾ tsp. salt
⅛ tsp. cayenne pepper
5 tomatoes, quartered, or
20 small cherry tomatoes
3 green peppers, cut into
20 chunks
¼ cup melted pareve
margarine

Place gefilte fish and mushrooms in a 12-inch × 8-inch × 1¾-inch glass dish. Combine salad oil, Worcestershire sauce, lemon juice, parsley, salt, and cayenne pepper; pour over gefilte fish and mushrooms. Cover with plastic wrap; refrigerate for 30 minutes, turning fish balls and mushrooms once.

On wooden skewers, alternate gefilte fish balls, mushrooms, tomato, and green pepper. Place 4 kabobs in a glass dish. Brush with melted pareve margarine. Microwave for 4 minutes on 50 percent power or until cooked, turning and basting with margarine once. Serves four to six.

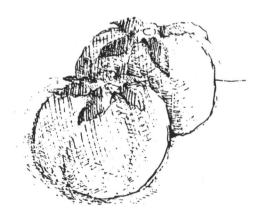

SNAPPER NOIR

1 tbsp. plain bread crumbs
1 tsp. dried basil
1 tsp. paprika
½ tsp. dried thyme
½ tsp. dried oregano
½ tsp. salt

½ tsp. ground pepper
¼ tsp. red pepper flakes
2 red snapper fillets (about
   1 inch thick)
½ tsp. corn oil
½ lime

Grind crumbs in food processor with remaining ingredients except fish fillets, oil, and lime until fine. Coat fillets with seasoned crumbs. Over high heat, heat a cast-iron skillet large enough to hold fish in one layer until very hot. Brush with oil. Place fish in skillet. Cook, turning once, 3 to 4 minutes on each side or until fish is crisp, golden, and slightly blackened in spots. Squeeze lime over fillets just before serving. Serves two.

NOTE; This recipe creates a great deal of smoke. Make sure your kitchen is well ventilated and use exhaust fans if possible.

STUFFED KRABETTES

¼ lb. plus 2 tbsp. butter or
   margarine
1 onion, minced
1 bell pepper, minced
1 garlic clove, minced
2 cups flaked smoked trout
   or whitefish
¾ cup seasoned bread
   crumbs

¼ cup water
juice of ½ lemon
1 tbsp. minced parsley
⅛ tsp. Worcestershire
   sauce
⅛ tsp. Tabasco sauce

In food processor fitted with metal blade, process onion, bell pepper, and garlic until finely chopped or minced. In a large skillet, melt ¼ pound butter or margarine over medium heat. Sauté onion, bell pepper, and garlic until lightly browned. Add fish, ½ cup bread crumbs, water, and lemon juice. Cook over low heat for about 20 minutes. Add parsley, Worcestershire sauce, and Tabasco. Place in 8 aluminum crab shells or 8 shell-shaped ramekins. Sprinkle with remaining bread crumbs and dot with remaining butter or margarine. Brown quickly in preheated 450-degree oven for only a few minutes or they will burn. Makes eight.

TIGER ISLAND TUNA

4 10-oz. pkgs. frozen
    chopped spinach
2 10-oz. pkgs. frozen
    artichoke hearts
¼ lb. plus 1 tbsp. butter
1 medium onion, chopped
1 bunch shallots, chopped
1 green pepper, chopped

2 tbsp. lemon juice
1 8-oz. pkg. cream cheese
2 sprigs parsley, minced
⅓ cup seasoned bread
    crumbs
salt and pepper to taste
3 6½-oz. cans tuna fish,
    drained and flaked

Cook spinach and artichokes according to package directions. In food processor fitted with metal blade, process onion, shallots, and green pepper until chopped. Sauté vegetables in ¼ pound butter until golden and limp. Add spinach and 1 tablespoon lemon juice. Add cream cheese and stir until smooth. Add parsley, ¼ cup bread crumbs (enough to absorb the butter), and salt and pepper to taste.

Grease a 2-quart casserole. Arrange artichoke hearts on bottom, top with tuna fish and then the spinach mixture. Dot with remaining butter, bread crumbs, and lemon juice. Bake in a 350-degree oven for about 30 minutes or until top is brown. Serves six to eight.

TRAYFISH BEIGNETS

1 cup all-purpose flour
1 tsp. baking powder
1 cup water
2 cloves garlic, chopped
1 pimento, chopped
3 shallots, with tops,
  chopped

1/8 tsp. Tabasco sauce
1/2 lb. smoked trout,
  skinned, boned, and
  flaked into large pieces
vegetable oil for deep frying

In food processor fitted with metal blade, process garlic, pimento, and shallots until well chopped but not ground.

In a bowl, mix flour, baking powder, water, chopped vegetables, and Tabasco sauce. Fold flaked fish into batter. Cover bowl with damp towel and set aside for 30 minutes to allow batter to thicken.

Heat oil in a deep skillet until it reaches 325° F. Drop fish batter by spoonfuls into oil and fry until golden brown, about 7 to 8 minutes. Drain and serve hot with lemon wedges or seafood sauce, if desired. Makes about two dozen.

TRIPP'S TUNA WEDGES

2 eggs
1 1/2 cups cooked rice
6 shallots, with tops, finely
  chopped
2 6 1/2-oz. cans tuna fish,
  undrained

1/2 cup butter
1/4 tsp. thyme
1/8 tsp. Worcestershire
  sauce
1 cup seasoned bread
  crumbs

In a large mixing bowl beat eggs with fork. Add rice, chopped shallots, and undrained tuna. Mix well.

Place butter in a small glass bowl. Microwave on High for 1 minute until melted. Add to tuna along with thyme, Worcestershire sauce, and bread crumbs. Mix well. Spread mixture evenly in a lightly greased

9-inch pie plate. Cover with wax paper. Microwave on High for 9 to 10 minutes, rotating dish a half-turn after 5 minutes. Serve in wedges. Serves six.

TROUT FILLED TO THE GILLS

2 whole trout (about ½ lb. each), cleaned and gutted
2 ribs celery, chopped
2 shallots, with tops, chopped
½ green pepper, chopped
1 clove garlic, chopped
¼ cup butter or margarine

½ cup seasoned bread crumbs
¼ tsp. lemon pepper
¼ tsp. Worcestershire sauce
1 tbsp. butter or margarine
2 tsp. lemon juice

In food processor fitted with steel blade, process celery, shallots, garlic, and green pepper until coarsely chopped.

In a 1-quart casserole, combine celery, shallots, green pepper, garlic, and ¼ cup butter or margarine. Cover; microwave on High for 2 to 3 minutes or until vegetables are tender. Stir in bread crumbs, lemon pepper, and Worcestershire sauce. Stuff trout, secure with wooden picks, and place in an 8-inch × 8-inch baking dish.

In a small dish melt 1 tablespoon butter or margarine on High (15 to 30 seconds). Mix in lemon juice. Brush fish with lemon butter. Cover dish with wax paper. Microwave on High for 5 to 6 minutes or until fish flakes easily, turning and brushing with lemon butter after half the time. Serves two.

VEGGIE-LOX PASTA

1½ sticks butter
2 cloves garlic, minced
1 small eggplant, halved
   and thinly sliced
4 large mushrooms, sliced
¼ tsp. garlic powder
½ tsp. white pepper
½ tsp. onion powder
½ tsp. cayenne pepper
½ tsp. paprika

½ tsp. dried thyme
¼ tsp. black pepper
1 medium zucchini, thinly
   sliced
½ cup coarsely chopped
   lox
1 lb. spaghetti, cooked
   al dente
about ¼ cup grated
   Parmesan cheese

In a large skillet melt ½ stick butter and sauté garlic. Add remaining butter, eggplant, mushrooms, and all the seasonings. Sauté for 2 minutes. Add zucchini and cook until vegetables are tender. Reduce heat to low. Add lox and heat thoroughly. Arrange vegetables mixed with lox over cooked spaghetti. Top with any remaining garlic butter from skillet and sprinkle with Parmesan cheese. Serves four.

Thibodaux
MEAT

"The Gateway to Bayou Country" is an apt name for Thibodaux. A picturesque community, founded on Bayou Lafourche in 1820, it offers both Southern charm and well-known Cajun hospitality. Street-signs in both French and English direct the native and tourist through the town.

Strategically situated on the bayou, Thibodaux was a natural gathering place, where Cajuns living in the area brought their crops for trading and shipping. As the town grew, it became a trading post for the bayou communities and cities like New Orleans. Thibodaux's unique appeal is its Cajun heritage. Weekend festivals and Mardi Gras parades are a longstanding tradition. The Volunteer Fireman's Parade, which dates back to 1857, and the "Firemen's Fair," for example, continue to finance the volunteer fire department.

Thibodaux embraces all the beauty, history, and Cajun culture for which this part of Louisiana is famous. There are moss-laden oaks, fields of sugar cane, and plantation homes along the bayou. Thibodaux is home to musicians, Confederate heroes, state congressmen, and Jim Bowie of Alamo fame. Even the architecture is a beautiful blending of past and present, where early nineteenth century buildings stand alongside those of the most modern design. The Laurel Valley Plantation, a few miles from Thibodaux, is a National Historic Landmark. The plantation is the site of the largest, most intact turn-of-the-century sugar plantation complex in the Southern United States. Culturally, Thibodaux boasts over 15,000 descendants of French-Canadian settlers, Cajuns whose preserved traditions uniquely color the community.

Today, Thibodaux is a modern, progressive metropolis. Its rich land supports sugar cane farming, factories, and the oil industry. The modern civic center brings cultural events to town and modern hotels and motels accommodate conventions and visitors.

It is especially in the realm of food that Thibodaux exemplifies its slogan, "Where Yesterday Welcomes Tomorrow." The food you will find here reflects Thibodaux's versatility. On one end of the street may be a fast-food outlet, while on the other, a restaurant steeped in Cajun folklore, serving the authentic Cajun food of the original settlers. The residents extend you an invitation to come to see and taste it all. "Allons à Thibodaux" – Come on to Thibodaux!

MEAT

Bar-B-Q'd Eve's Ribs *(Conventional)*
Big Maxie Burger *(Microwave)*
Braised Adam's Ribs *(Conventional)*
A Brisk Brisket *(Conventional)*
Certainly! Stuffed Peppers *(Microwave)*
Chops for the Cajun *(Processor and Conventional)*
Glacé Brisket *(Conventional)*
Herb-ette's Lamb Chops *(Conventional)*
King Kajun Burger *(Conventional)*
Spice Mix *(Conventional)*
Laurel Valley Meat Loaf *(Microwave)*
Lazar's Loaf *(Processor and Conventional)*
Leola's Lamb Shoulder – Stuffed *(Processor and Conventional)*
Liver You'll Like *(Microwave and Conventional)*
Mercedes' Meat Pie *(Conventional)*
Pastry *(Conventional)*
Pelican Pot Roast *(Microwave and Conventional)*
Simmering Stew *(Conventional)*
Simply Stuffed Peppers *(Processor and Conventional)*
Spicy Franks from Thibodaux *(Microwave and Conventional)*
Veal Pie from Verna *(Conventional)*
Vorscht un Luckshen (Sausage and Spaghetti)
        (Processor and Conventional)

BAR-B-Q'D EVE'S RIBS

3 lbs. short ribs of beef
2 onions, thinly sliced
½ cup ketchup
1½ tsp. salt

¼ tsp. Tabasco sauce
⅛ tsp. chili powder
1 cup water

Put half of the short ribs in a heavy pot and cover with a layer of onion slices. Combine ketchup, salt, Tabasco sauce, chili powder, and water. Pour half of this mixture over meat and onions. Repeat with another layer of short ribs, sliced onion, and sauce. Cover and bake in a preheated 325-degree oven for about 2 hours or until ribs are tender. Serves four to six.

BIG MAXIE BURGER

1 lb. ground beef
½ tsp. seasoned salt

1 tsp. Kitchen Bouquet
1 tsp. water

Mix salt into ground meat and shape into four patties 4 inches across and ½ inch thick. Arrange patties in a 9-inch square glass baking dish. Brush tops of hamburgers with Kitchen Bouquet diluted with water. Cook in microwave at 50 percent power (Medium) for 2 minutes. Turn and brush other side with drippings. Cook 3 minutes longer at 50 percent power. Cooking time can be adjusted depending upon desired degree of doneness. Total cooking time of 5 minutes is for well-done hamburgers. Serves four.

BRAISED ADAM'S RIBS

2 lbs. short ribs of beef
1 tsp. salt
¼ tsp. cayenne pepper
¼ tsp. powdered thyme
½ tsp. garlic powder
3 tbsp. flour

2 tbsp. vegetable
  shortening
½ cup water
4 small onions
4 medium potatoes
4 medium carrots

Cut ribs into 2-inch pieces. Mix seasonings with flour and rub flour mixture into ribs. Brown in melted shortening. Arrange ribs in greased baking dish. Add water to pan in which meat was browned; stir with drippings and pour over meat. Cover and bake in a preheated 325-degree oven for about 2 hours. Add onions, potatoes, carrots and more water if necessary. Return to oven and bake, covered, for about 1 hour. Serves four.

A BRISK BRISKET

1 3- to 4-lb. brisket roast
¼ tsp. salt
¼ tsp. pepper
¼ tsp. garlic powder

1 tsp. minced onion
1 tbsp. Worcestershire
  sauce

Place roast in a small roasting pan. Sprinkle with salt, pepper, garlic powder, onion, and Worcestershire sauce. Cover with aluminum foil and roast in a preheated 350-degree oven for about 3½ hours or until tender. Slice thinly against the grain of the meat. Serves four to six.

CERTAINLY! STUFFED PEPPERS

6 medium bell peppers
1 tbsp. pareve margarine
1 cup chopped onions
¼ cup chopped parsley
¼ tsp. garlic powder
½ tsp. black pepper
¼ cup bread crumbs or
  cooked rice

1 egg, beaten
6 cups cooked and minced
  meat, such as chicken,
  lamb, veal or ground beef
½ beef bouillon cube
½ cup water

Cut bell peppers in half crosswise, remove seeds, and cut off stems. Set aside.

In a 2-quart bowl, combine margarine, onion, parsley, garlic powder, and black pepper. Microwave on High for 2 to 3 minutes or until soft but not brown. Add bread crumbs or rice, egg, and cooked meat. Dissolve bouillon cube in water. Add ¼ cup bouillon liquid to meat mixture. Mix well.

Stuff bell peppers and place in an 8-inch × 12-inch microwave-safe baking dish. Spoon remaining bouillon over bell peppers. Cover with plastic wrap. Microwave on High for 6 minutes; rearrange. Microwave on High for 6 minutes more or until bell pepper is tender and meat mixture is hot. Let stand, covered, for 5 minutes before serving. Serves six.

CHOPS FOR THE CAJUN

6 veal chops, cut ½ inch
  thick
1½ tsp. garlic powder
1½ tsp. thyme
1½ tsp. salt
¾ tsp. cumin
¼ tsp. cayenne pepper

1 10-oz. can kosher
  condensed chicken soup
1 cup long-grain white rice
1 stalk celery, chopped
4 shallots, with tops,
  chopped
½ red pepper, chopped

Combine garlic powder, thyme, salt, cumin, and cayenne pepper. Sprinkle half of spice mixture over one side of chops. Rub into meat. Repeat on reverse side of chops, using remaining spice mixture. Add enough water to chicken soup to make 2 cups liquid.

In a 10-inch skillet, combine liquid and rice; mix well. Arrange chops over rice, overlapping if necessary. Bring to a boil. Reduce heat, cover tightly, and simmer for 20 minutes.

In food processor fitted with metal blade, process celery, shallots, and red pepper until coarsely chopped. Add vegetables to skillet. Continue to cook until all liquid is absorbed and rice is tender and fluffy. Serves six.

GLACÉ BRISKET

4- to 5-lb. boneless beef
  brisket
juice from 1-qt. jar of
  kosher-style dill pickles

½ cup brown sugar
2 tbsp. prepared mustard
½ tsp. Worcestershire
  sauce

Marinate roast in pickle juice for 48 hours in refrigerator. Drain off juice and place roast in a baking pan. Cover and bake at 325° F. for 3 hours. Uncover roast, combine brown sugar, mustard, and Worcestershire sauce, and put on roast. Return roast to oven and bake 1 hour longer. Baste occasionally. Serves six to eight.

HERB-ETTE'S LAMB CHOPS

1 egg, slightly beaten
1 tsp. salt
½ tsp. pepper
2 tsp. finely chopped
  parsley
½ tsp. powdered rosemary

½ tsp. powdered thyme
8 rib lamb chops, 1 to 1½
  inches thick, well
  trimmed
4 tbsp. pareve margarine

In a bowl, mix well egg, salt, pepper, parsley, rosemary, and thyme. Brush both sides of chops with mixture. Cover and let stand 1 hour at room temperature. In a large heavy skillet, melt the margarine and cook chops for 8 minutes on each side or until desired degree of doneness is reached. Serves four.

KING KAJUN BURGER

2 tbsp. vegetable oil
2½ tsp. spice mix (see
  recipe below)
2 medium onions, cut into
  ½-inch slices
1 large green pepper, cut
  into ½-inch slices

1 tsp. chopped garlic
2 tbsp. melted pareve
  margarine
4 hamburger buns
1½ lbs. ground beef

Preheat broiler. In a large skillet heat oil with 2 teaspoons spice mix. Add onions, green pepper, and chopped garlic. Cover and cook, stirring occasionally, for 15 minutes or until tender.

Combine margarine with ½ teaspoon spice mix. Split hamburger buns and brush cut sides with seasoned margarine. Broil on cookie sheet until toasted; set aside.

Divide ground meat into 4 patties. Coat each side evenly with remaining spice mixture. Broil about 4 inches from heat for about 3 to 5 minutes, depending upon degree of doneness desired. Place patties on toasted rolls and top with sautéed onion and pepper mixture. Serves four.

Spice Mix

1¼ tsp. salt
1 tsp. freshly ground black
  pepper
¼ tsp. ground red pepper

1½ tsp. paprika
1¼ tsp. thyme
1¼ tsp. basil

Combine all spices in a small bowl. Makes 2 heaping tablespoons.

LAUREL VALLEY MEAT LOAF

1½ lbs. ground beef
1 egg, slightly beaten
2 tsp. salt
½ cup nondairy creamer
¼ cup water
1 cup bread crumbs

2 tbsp. minced onion
½ cup finely chopped
  celery
2 tbsp. ketchup
2 slices Beef Frye

Mix together all ingredients except ketchup and Beef Frye just until blended. Pack mixture in an 8½-inch × 4½-inch × 3-inch ovenware loaf dish. Spread ketchup on top and cover with Beef Frye. Cover with waxed paper.

Set control at "Bake." Microwave for 33 minutes or until done. Allow meat loaf to stand 10 minutes before serving. Serves six.

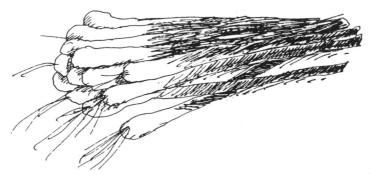

LAZAR'S LOAF

1 lb. ground beef
2 eggs, well beaten
1 tsp. salt
¼ tsp. garlic powder
¼ tsp. black pepper
4 sprigs parsley, finely
   chopped

1 small onion, finely
   chopped
1 tbsp. Worcestershire
   sauce
1 cup bread crumbs

In food processor fitted with metal blade, process parsley and onion until finely chopped. Combine parsley and onion with all other ingredients; mix well. Pack in a lightly greased loaf pan. Bake at 350° F. for 1 hour or until well done. Serves four.

LEOLA'S LAMB SHOULDER –
STUFFED

1 4-lb. shoulder of lamb
1 tbsp. pareve margarine
2 bay leaves, crushed
1 onion, finely chopped
1 green pepper, finely
   chopped

2 large tomatoes, finely
   chopped
1 tsp. salt
1 cup cooked rice

Have shoulder of lamb boned to make a pocket for stuffing. In food processor, process onion and green pepper until finely chopped. Remove and set aside. Process tomatoes until finely chopped and set aside.

Melt margarine in a heavy skillet. Add bay leaves, onion, and green pepper and cook until tender. Add chopped tomatoes and salt and cook for 5 minutes. Stir in rice. Fill pocket of lamb with mixture. Fasten with skewers or tie with heavy string. Place on a rack in a baking pan, fat side up. Bake in a 325-degree oven for about 2½ hours or until done. Serves four.

LIVER YOU'LL LIKE

1 lb. calf's liver, cut into
  strips
1 onion, sliced
1 green pepper, sliced
2 stalks celery, sliced
1 clove garlic, minced
4 slices Beef Frye, diced
1 16-oz. can stewed
  tomatoes

1 10-oz. pkg. frozen sliced
  okra
1 bay leaf
1¼ tsp. salt
water
2 tbsp. all-purpose flour
½ tsp. chili powder
½ tsp. thyme
¼ tsp. pepper

Place liver under conventional broiler and singe for ½ minute on each side. Remove and set aside.

MICROWAVE: Place onion, green pepper, celery, garlic, and Beef Frye in a 4-quart casserole. Cover tightly with plastic wrap, turning back edge to vent. Microwave at 100 percent power for 8 minutes, stirring once. Add tomatoes, okra, bay leaf, ¼ teaspoon salt, and ½ cup water. Cover, leaving vent, and microwave at 100 percent power for 13 minutes. Mix flour, chili powder, thyme, pepper, and remaining salt. Coat liver with flour mixture. Add liver to tomato mixture. Cover and microwave at 70 percent power for 14 minutes, stirring twice, until liver is fork-tender. Remove bay leaf and adjust seasoning if necessary. Serves four to six.

CONVENTIONAL: Sauté onion, green pepper, celery, garlic, and Beef Frye in a large skillet until onion is transparent, about 10 minutes. Add tomatoes, okra, bay leaf, ¼ teaspoon salt, and 1 cup water. Heat to boiling. Reduce heat, cover, and simmer for 15 minutes. Mix flour, chili powder, thyme, pepper, and remaining salt. Coat liver with flour mixture. Add liver to tomato mixture. Cover and simmer for 15 minutes or until liver is fork-tender. Serves four to six.

MERCEDES' MEAT PIE

2½ lbs. ground beef
2 tbsp. flour
2 tbsp. vegetable
    shortening
2 large onions, chopped

2 tbsp. chopped parsley
salt and pepper to taste
oil for deep frying

Make a roux of shortening and flour. Add other ingredients and salt and pepper to taste. Cook thoroughly until meat is no longer pink and onions are limp. Let cool before placing in pastry dough.

Pastry

4 cups flour
2 tsp. baking powder
1 tsp. salt
2 eggs

½ cup melted vegetable
    shortening
nondairy creamer

Sift together flour, baking powder, and salt. Add shortening, then eggs. Add enough nondairy creamer to make a stiff dough. Roll very thin. Using a large circular pastry cutter or saucer, cut 18 circles of dough. Half-fill with meat mixture (about a tablespoon). Fold dough over, dampen edges with water, and crimp closed with a fork. Fry in deep fat until golden brown. Makes eighteen.

PELICAN POT ROAST

1 onion, sliced
1 stalk celery, sliced
2 tbsp. pareve margarine
1 2½- to 3-lb. boneless
  chuck roast
1 beef bouillon cube
½ tsp. oregano

½ tsp. thyme
1 tsp. salt
¼ tsp. ground pepper
6 potatoes, peeled and
  halved
6 carrots, cut into 1-inch
  chunks

MICROWAVE: Combine onion, celery, and margarine in a 4-quart casserole. Cover tightly with plastic wrap, turning back edge to vent. Microwave at 100 percent power for 4 minutes. Add meat, bouillon cube dissolved in 1 cup water, oregano, thyme, salt, and pepper. Cover, leaving vent, and microwave at 100 percent power for 5 minutes. Reduce power to 50 percent and microwave for 20 minutes. Turn meat over, add potatoes, carrots, and a small amount of liquid if necessary. Cover and microwave at 50 percent power for 40 minutes or until meat is fork-tender, stirring twice. Let stand, covered, for 5 minutes. Remove meat to warm platter and arrange vegetables around meat. Skim excess fat from cooking liquid, adjust seasonings, and pour into gravy boat. Serves six to eight.

CONVENTIONAL: Sauté onion and celery in margarine in a Dutch oven. Push vegetables to one side. Add meat and brown lightly on each side. Stir in beef bouillon cube dissolved in 1½ cups water, oregano, thyme, salt, and pepper. Heat to boiling. Reduce heat, cover, and simmer 1½ hours. Add potatoes, carrots, and more liquid if necessary. Cover and simmer for 30 minutes longer or until meat and vegetables are fork-tender. Remove meat to warm platter and arrange vegetables around meat. Skim excess fat from cooking liquid, adjust seasonings, and pour into gravy boat. Serves six to eight.

SIMMERING STEW

1½ lbs. beef chuck
¼ cup flour
¼ cup pareve margarine
1 cup sliced onion
2 large cloves of garlic,
  minced
¼ cup chopped parsley
1 tbsp. salt
⅛ tsp. pepper
1 bay leaf

1 tbsp. Worcestershire
  sauce
2 cups cubed potatoes
1½ cups 1-inch carrot
  strips
1 cup sliced celery
½ cup chopped green
  pepper
1 cup sliced fresh
  mushrooms

Trim and cut the beef into 1-inch cubes, then coat with flour. Melt margarine in a Dutch oven or large heavy saucepan. Add beef and brown well on all sides. Remove beef and set aside. Cook onion and garlic in margarine until onion is tender. Return beef to pan and add 2 cups water, parsley, salt, pepper, bay leaf, and Worcestershire sauce. Cover and simmer for 1 hour, stirring occasionally and adding more water if needed. Add potatoes, carrots, celery, and green pepper and cover. Simmer for 15 minutes longer, then add mushrooms. Cover and simmer for an additional 10 minutes. Serves four to five.

SIMPLY STUFFED PEPPERS

1½ lbs. ground beef
1 small onion, chopped
2 shallots, with tops,
  chopped
½ bell pepper, chopped
¼ cup vegetable oil
½ cup bread crumbs

¼ tsp. oregano
¼ tsp. dried parsley
salt and pepper to taste
1 egg, beaten
1 tsp. Worcestershire sauce
6 large bell peppers
pareve margarine

In food processor fitted with metal blade, process onion, shallots with tops, and bell pepper until finely chopped. Sauté ground meat, onions, shallots, and bell pepper in oil until meat is brown. Add bread crumbs and seasonings. Let cool slightly. Add beaten egg and Worcestershire sauce.

Slice tops off peppers and remove seeds. Stuff mixture into peppers and sprinkle with additional bread crumbs. Dot with pareve margarine. Bake at 350° F. for 20 to 25 minutes or until tops are brown. Serves six.

SPICY FRANKS FROM THIBODAUX

1 large green pepper, cut into ½-inch pieces
1 large onion, coarsely diced
2 tbsp. vegetable oil (for conventional method only)
1 16-oz. can baked beans, with liquid
1 16-oz. can whole kernel corn, drained

1 8-oz. can tomato sauce
2 tbsp. prepared mustard
2 tsp. chili powder
1 lb. kosher frankfurters, cut into ½-inch pieces
¼ cup grated pareve imitation cheese (optional)

MICROWAVE: Combine green pepper and onion in a 2-quart glass bowl or casserole. Cover tightly with plastic wrap, turning back edge to vent. Microwave at 100 percent power for 3 minutes. Stir in beans, corn, tomato sauce, mustard, and chili powder. Add frankfurters and stir to combine. Cover, leaving vent, and microwave at 90 percent power for 11 minutes, stirring twice. Uncover and top with imitation cheese, if desired. Microwave at 90 percent power for 1 minute to melt cheese. Let stand for 5 minutes before serving. Serves six.

CONVENTIONAL: Lightly grease a 2-quart casserole. Preheat oven to 350° F. Sauté green pepper and onion in oil in skillet until onion is transparent, about 5 minutes. Stir in beans, corn, tomato sauce, chili powder, and mustard. Add frankfurters and stir to combine. Pour into prepared casserole. Bake for 25 minutes or until hot and bubbly. Arrange imitation cheese over top of casserole, if desired, and bake for 5 minutes longer to melt cheese and brown lightly. Serves six.

VEAL PIE FROM VERNA

1½ lbs. veal, cut into cubes
3 tbsp. vegetable
  shortening
3 tbsp. flour
1 medium onion, chopped
1 carrot, sliced
1 medium potato, diced

2 cups water
1 tsp. salt
⅛ tsp. pepper
2 hard-cooked eggs,
  chopped
1 recipe pareve pie pastry

In a skillet brown veal in vegetable shortening and stir in flour. Add onion, carrot, potato, water, and seasonings and cook over medium heat until thick. Place half veal mixture in a 10-inch × 6½-inch baking dish and cover with eggs. Add remaining veal mixture. Cover with pastry and make 3 or 4 slits in top crust. Bake at 350° F. for 1 hour or until top of pie is brown and crisp. Serves six to eight.

VORSCHT UN LUCKSHEN
(Sausage and Spaghetti)

1 lb. kosher smoked
  sausages
2 green peppers, chopped
2 medium onions, chopped
2 15-oz. cans tomato sauce
1 6-oz. can tomato paste
1 4-oz. can sliced
  mushrooms, with liquid

1 tbsp. Worcestershire
  sauce
1 tsp. basil leaves, crushed
1 tsp. salt
¼ tsp. pepper
⅛ tsp. garlic powder
1 lb. spaghetti

In a large skillet fry sausages until almost brown. Cut green peppers and discard seeds. In food processor fitted with metal blade, process peppers and onions until coarsely chopped. Add pepper and onion mixture to sausages and cook until tender. Stir in tomato sauce, tomato paste, mushrooms with liquid, Worcestershire sauce, and remaining seasonings. Simmer uncovered for 20 minutes.

Prepare spaghetti according to package directions. Drain well. Arrange spaghetti on large platter and pour sauce over top. Serves six to eight.

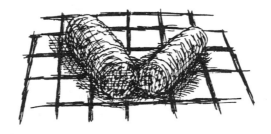

Bayou Lafourche
DESSERTS

Bayou Lafourche is one of Louisiana's most famous and picturesque bayous. Most of the communities of Lafourche Parish cling to the shores of Bayou Lafourche. In French, Lafourche means "the fork." The name was originally given to Bayou Lafourche because of the fork formed where the bayou flows out of the Mississippi River in Donaldsonville. In the early days of the settlers, the waterways, especially Bayou Lafourche, provided the chief means of transportation. The Bayou's channel stretches the length of Lafourche Parish and connects the Mississippi River to the Gulf of Mexico. The Cajuns who live along its banks call it their main street, "The Longest 'Street' in the World."

The towns and villages dotting the area have strange but intriguing names. Lockport, Larose, and Cut Off are towns that rely on the bayou for their boat building industries. Galliano and Golden Meadow are oil and fishing centers. Golden Meadow was named for the profusion of goldenrod that grows in the fields – meadows that cover pools of oil and natural gas. Grand Isle is considered one of the ten best fishing spots in the world. It is said there is more parking for boats than for cars in this area. Port Fourchon, at the mouth of the bayou on the Gulf of Mexico, is famous for housing America's only Superport – a deep-water pumping terminal for huge tankers that travel the world.

Bayou Lafourche brings together all that is genuinely Cajun and Southern in south Louisiana. Visiting the surrounding areas is like taking in a bit of yesterday. Cajun French, Cajun humor, and Cajun food are everywhere. As you travel along the bayou, each community has something different to offer, but best of all are the warm and interesting people. At every town and village, the tourist can find a pot of coffee, a bowl of gumbo, the best homemade beignets, pies, and French bread, and always a lively, often animated, conversation with the natives.

Cajuns love life and live it to the fullest. Through the labor of their hands and their love of life, these people created an Eden on Bayou Lafourche. As one wanders up and down the bayou, one can readily understand why both natives and tourists refer to it as a Cajun paradise.

Yes, there is something for everyone along Bayou Lafourche, all because of the people who live here. The Cajuns are spirited people. They work hard and play hard. They revel in celebrations – many celebrations. From April through October not a weekend goes by without a fair, festival, parade, fishing rodeo, or food fest. More than fifty such events take place up and down the bayou each year; at each you are likely to find a sample of their food and you can hear the Cajun chefs, in their own inimitable way, saying: "Allons manger" – let's eat!

DESSERTS

Bayou Lafourche Bread Pudding *(Conventional)*
Whiskey Sauce *(Conventional)*
"Bla-a- 🎵 -k Berry" Dumplings *(Conventional)*
Bubba's Banana Muffins *(Microwave and Conventional)*
Cecily's Coconut Cake *(Conventional)*
Coconut Filling and Frosting *(Conventional)*
Channel Carrot Cake *(Microwave and Conventional)*
Pineapple Cream Cheese Frosting *(Conventional)*
Fudge à la Fourchon *(Microwave and Conventional)*
Galliano Glazed Pecans *(Microwave)*
Golden Meadow Coffee Cake *(Processor and Conventional)*
Lemon Cake LaRose *(Processor and Conventional)*
Lemon Glaze *(Conventional)*
Lockport Lemon Pie *(Microwave)*
Meringue *(Microwave)*
Mil's Lemon Meringue Pie *(Conventional)*
Paradise Pecan Pralines *(Microwave)*
Parish Pastry Shell *(Microwave, Conventional and Processor)*
Petit Pecan Cookies *(Conventional and Processor)*
Pinky's Chocolate Pecan Pie *(Conventional)*
Praline Powder *(Processor and Conventional)*
Purr-Fec Pralines *(Conventional)*
Rum Bread Pudding *(Microwave)*
Rum Sauce *(Microwave)*
Shuk-a-lot-Cake *(Microwave and Conventional)*
Chocolate Cream Frosting *(Microwave and Conventional)*
Sucré Almonds *(Conventional)*
Superport Strawberry Pie *(Microwave)*
Syl's Strawberry Pie *(Conventional)*
Très Bon Cherries Jubilee *(Microwave and Conventional)*

BAYOU LAFOURCHE
BREAD PUDDING

1 loaf stale French bread
(about 18 inches long)
1 qt. milk
4 eggs
2 cups sugar
½ tsp. cinnamon

2 tbsp. vanilla extract
1 cup seedless raisins
2 apples, peeled, cored,
and sliced
½ cup chopped pecans
¼ cup butter

Break bread into milk and allow to soak well. Beat eggs and add to bread and milk. Combine sugar, cinnamon, vanilla, raisins, apples, and nuts. Add to bread mixture. Mix well. Melt butter and pour into a 13-inch × 9-inch × 2-inch baking pan. Add the bread mixture. Bake about 50 minutes in a preheated 350-degree oven or until pudding is set and firm. Serve with Whiskey Sauce (see recipe). Serves twelve to fifteen.

WHISKEY SAUCE

1 stick butter, melted
1 cup sugar

1 egg, beaten
¼ cup whiskey

Cream butter and sugar in a double boiler. Add egg and stir rapidly to prevent curdling. Allow to cool. Add whiskey and pour over bread pudding. Makes one scant cup.

"BLA-A- ♪ -K BERRY" DUMPLINGS

4 tbsp. butter, melted
1 cup milk
2 eggs
3½ cups sugar
2 tsp. vanilla extract

3½ cups flour
3 tsp. baking powder
4 cups water
1½ qts. blackberries

Mix together melted butter, milk, eggs, 1 cup sugar, and vanilla. Stir in flour and baking powder, taking care not to overmix batter.

Combine water, remaining sugar, and blackberries. Cook over medium heat until mixture thickens. Drop batter by the spoonful into blackberry mixture and cook over medium heat until dough rises. Cook only until a fork inserted into dough comes out clean.

Remove dumplings and continue adding batter by the spoonful until all the batter is used. Serve warm, in dessert bowls, spooning remaining blackberry mixture over dumplings. Makes three to four dozen.

BUBBA'S BANANA MUFFINS

1¾ cups unsifted all-
  purpose flour
3 tsp. baking powder
½ tsp. salt
1 egg
¾ cup mashed banana
  (about 2 medium-size
  bananas)

½ cup milk
¼ cup vegetable oil
½ cup maple syrup
½ cup brown sugar
¼ cup chopped pecans

MICROWAVE: Place 2 paper cupcake liners in each cup of a 6-cup microwave-safe muffin pan. In a large bowl, stir together flour, baking powder, and salt. In a medium-size bowl, lightly beat egg. Stir in mashed banana, milk, oil, and maple syrup. Pour liquid ingredients all at once into dry ingredients. Stir mixture with fork until all ingredients are moistened, but do not overstir. Batter should look lumpy. Spoon scant ¼ cup batter into each cup. Combine brown sugar and chopped pecans. Using half of the mixture, sprinkle over tops of 6 muffins. Microwave, uncovered, at 100 percent power for 3½ to 4 minutes or until tops spring back when lightly touched with fingertip. Remove muffins from cups to wire rack to cool. Repeat to make 6 more muffins. Makes twelve.

CONVENTIONAL: Preheat oven to 400° F. Grease bottoms only of twelve 2½-inch muffin pan cups (or use paper liners). In a large bowl, stir together flour, baking powder, and salt. In a medium-size bowl, lightly beat egg. Stir in mashed banana, milk, oil, and maple syrup. Pour liquid ingredients all at once into dry ingredients. Stir mixture briskly with fork until all ingredients are moistened; do not overstir. Batter should be lumpy. Fill each prepared muffin cup ⅔ full with batter. Combine brown sugar and chopped pecans. Sprinkle tops of muffins with mixture. Bake in preheated 400° oven for 22 to 24 minutes. Remove pan to wire rack. Remove muffins at once and serve while still hot. Makes twelve.

CECILY'S COCONUT CAKE

½ lb. butter
2 cups sugar, sifted
5 eggs, separated
3 cups sifted flour
3 tsp. baking powder
½ tsp. salt

1 cup milk or 1 cup
  coconut milk
1 tsp. vanilla extract
Coconut Filling and
  Frosting (see recipe)

In a large bowl, cream butter well. Add sugar gradually and continue beating well until mixture is light and fluffy. Beat egg yolks until thick and lemon colored. Combine sifted flour, baking powder, and salt. Sift together three times. Add egg yolks to the butter mixture then alternately add flour mixture and milk. Beat after each addition.

Beat egg whites until stiff. Fold egg whites and vanilla into batter. Pour batter into three 9-inch greased and floured cake pans. Bake in a preheated 375-degree oven for 25 to 30 minutes or until cake recedes from edges of pan and is spongy to the touch. Cool on rack before removing from pans. When completely cool, fill and frost cake with Coconut Frosting (see recipe). Serves eight to ten.

COCONUT FILLING
AND FROSTING

2 cups grated fresh coconut
1½ cups sugar

1 cup evaporated milk
4 tbsp. butter

Cook coconut, 1 cup sugar, evaporated milk, and butter for 10 minutes on low heat. Use ⅓ of this mixture for filling. In a small skillet over low heat, brown the remaining sugar and add to remaining mixture. Use this to frost top and sides of cake. Makes enough for one 9-inch 3-layer cake.

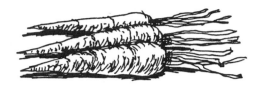

CHANNEL CARROT CAKE

1 cup all-purpose flour	1 egg
1 tsp. baking soda	⅓ cup vegetable oil
½ tsp. salt	¼ cup buttermilk (½ cup
1 tsp. cinnamon	for conventional method)
¼ tsp. nutmeg	1 cup shredded carrots
¼ tsp. cloves	¼ cup chopped nuts
1 cup firmly packed brown	Pineapple Cream Cheese
sugar	Frosting (see recipe)

MICROWAVE: Lightly grease an 8-inch round glass baking dish. Combine flour, baking soda, salt, cinnamon, nutmeg, and cloves. Beat sugar, egg, oil, and buttermilk until smooth and stir in carrots. Add carrot mixture and nuts to flour mixture. Stir just until moistened. Pour batter into prepared baking dish. Cover tightly with plastic wrap, turning back edge to vent. Microwave at 70 percent power for 8½ to 9 minutes or until surface of cake is fairly dry. (There will be a moist, partially cooked spot in the center of the cake.) Cool, covered with plastic wrap. When completely cool, remove cake from pan and spread with Pineapple Cream Cheese Frosting. Serves six.

CONVENTIONAL: Grease an 8-inch round baking dish. Preheat oven to 350° F. Combine flour, baking soda, salt, cinnamon, nutmeg, and cloves. Beat sugar, egg, oil, and ½ cup buttermilk until smooth and stir in carrots. Add carrot mixture and nuts to flour mixture. Stir just until moistened. Pour batter into prepared pan. Bake for 30 to 35 minutes or until center springs back when lightly pressed. Cool on wire rack. Remove cake from pan and spread with Pineapple Cream Cheese Frosting. Serves six.

PINEAPPLE CREAM CHEESE FROSTING

1 3-oz. pkg. cream cheese,
 softened
¼ cup crushed pineapple

dash salt
1¾ to 2 cups confectioners'
 sugar, sifted

Beat cream cheese, pineapple, and salt until well mixed. Add confectioners' sugar, beating until frosting is spreading consistency. Add additional sugar if necessary. Spread over cooled Carrot Cake. Makes enough for one 8-inch round or square cake.

FUDGE À LA FOURCHON

½ cup butter
¾ cup cocoa
4 cups confectioners' sugar,
 sifted
1 tsp. vanilla

½ cup evaporated milk
1 cup pecans, coarsely
 chopped
36 pecan halves (optional)

MICROWAVE: Microwave butter in a 2-quart microwave-safe bowl on 100 percent power for 1 to 1½ minutes or until melted. Add cocoa; stir until smooth. Stir in confectioners' sugar and vanilla. Blend well (mixture will be dry and crumbly). Stir in evaporated milk. Microwave on 100 percent power for 30 to 60 seconds or until mixture is hot. Stir until smooth; add chopped pecans. Pour into a foil-lined 9-inch-square pan. Cover and chill until firm. Cut into 1½-inch squares. Press pecan half into top of each square, if desired. Store, covered, in refrigerator. Makes thirty-six squares.

CONVENTIONAL: Melt butter in a medium saucepan. Remove from heat; stir in cocoa. Stir in confectioners' sugar and vanilla. Add evaporated milk. Stir constantly over low heat until warm and smooth. Add pecan pieces. Pour into a foil-lined 9-inch-square pan. Chill until firm. Cut into 1½-inch squares. Press pecan half into top of each square, if desired. Store, covered, in refrigerator. Makes thirty-six squares.

GALLIANO GLAZED PECANS

2 sticks butter
1 cup firmly packed brown
  sugar

1 tsp. cinnamon
4 cups pecan halves

Place butter in a 1½-quart microwave-safe casserole. Microwave on 70 percent power for 1 to 1½ minutes or until butter is melted. Stir in brown sugar and cinnamon. Microwave on 100 percent power for 2 minutes or until bubbly. Add nuts and mix to coat each piece evenly. Microwave on 100 percent power for 3 to 5 minutes or until hot and bubbly. Spread out onto wax paper and let cool slightly. Makes about one pound.

GOLDEN MEADOW COFFEE CAKE

1½ cups sour cream
1½ tsp. baking soda
¾ cup pecan halves
1¾ cups sugar
2 tsp. cinnamon
3 cups all-purpose flour
2 tsp. baking powder

1½ tsp. salt
3 large eggs
2 sticks unsalted butter at
  room temperature, cut
  into 8 pieces
2 tsp. vanilla extract

Stir baking soda into sour cream and let stand at room temperature for 30 minutes. Preheat oven to 350° F. Generously butter a 10-cup bundt pan.

Insert metal blade into food processor. Put in pecans, ½ cup sugar, and cinnamon and pulse about 4 times until pecans are coarsely chopped. Remove mixture from bowl and set aside.

Put flour, baking powder, and salt in bowl and process for 3 seconds to blend. Remove and set aside. Put eggs and remaining sugar in bowl and process for 1 minute, stopping once to scrape down the sides of the bowl. Add butter and vanilla and process for 1 minute, stopping once to scrape down the sides of the bowl. Add reserved flour mixture and pulse 4 or 5 times, just until flour disappears. Do not overprocess.

Pour ⅓ of batter into prepared bundt pan, then sprinkle surface with ⅓ of nut mixture. Add another layer of batter, then remaining nut mixture. Spread rest of batter over nuts and smooth with spatula. Bake in a preheated 350-degree oven for 1 hour or until toothpick inserted in center comes out clean. Let the cake cool in the pan for 5 minutes, then invert the pan onto a wire rack. Remove the pan and let the cake cool completely. Serves about twelve.

LEMON CAKE LaROSE

2 lemons
1 cup sugar
2 sticks unsalted butter
4 large eggs

1¾ cups all-purpose flour
2 tsp. baking powder
Lemon Glaze (see recipe)

Butter and flour a 6-cup ring mold or loaf pan, or two 3¾-cup loaf pans. Preheat oven to 325° F.

Remove peel from lemons using a vegetable peeler; cut peel into 2-inch pieces. In food processor with metal blade in place, combine lemon peel and sugar. Process until peel is finely chopped. Add butter and process until smooth, about 30 seconds. Add eggs and process until smooth, about 30 seconds. Scrape down sides of bowl with spatula as needed. Stir flour and baking powder together. Add to mixture and pulse on and off just until flour disappears. Do not over-process.

Transfer batter to prepared pan(s). Bake for 50 to 55 minutes or until toothpick inserted in center comes out clean. For large loaf pan, bake about 10 minutes longer. Let cool slightly in pan. Remove cake from pan and place on wire rack over wax paper. Spoon Lemon Glaze over top of cake. Repeat as cake cools, until all the glaze is used. When cool, wrap in plastic or foil and refrigerate. Makes one large or two small cakes.

LEMON GLAZE

1 cup sifted confectioners'
sugar

juice of ½ lemon

Mix together confectioners' sugar and lemon juice until blended. Spoon over top of cake and let drizzle down sides. Makes enough for one large or two small cakes.

LOCKPORT LEMON PIE

1 baked 9-inch pie shell
1½ cups sugar
⅓ cup cornstarch
1½ cups boiling water
3 egg yolks, slightly beaten

3 tbsp. butter or margarine
4 tbsp. lemon juice
1 tsp. grated lemon rind
Meringue (see recipe)

Mix sugar, cornstarch, and water together in a 1-quart glass casserole. Cook in microwave at 50 percent power for 2½ minutes. Stir. Cook 1 minute longer at 50 percent power or until thick, stirring after 30 seconds. Beat a little of hot mixture into egg yolks; then return to rest of mixture. Cook in microwave on 50 percent power for 30 seconds. Blend in butter or margarine, lemon juice, and rind. Cool. Pour into baked pie shell. Top with meringue, sealing meringue to edge of pie crust. Microwave on High for 2 to 3 minutes to set meringue. Or you may want to brown meringue in conventional oven. Serves eight.

MERINGUE

3 egg whites
¼ tsp. cream of tartar

¼ cup sugar

In a medium mixing bowl, combine egg whites and cream of tartar. Beat until foamy. Gradually add sugar and continue beating until stiff peaks form. Spread on pie.

MIL'S LEMON MERINGUE PIE

1 baked 9-inch pie shell
5 eggs, separated
¾ cup sugar
¼ cup lemon juice
1 tsp. lemon zest

2 tbsp. butter or margarine
6 tbsp. sugar
1 tsp. lemon zest
1 tsp. lemon juice

Beat egg yolks until thick and lemon colored. Add ¾ cup sugar, ¼ cup at a time, beating well with each addition. Add ¼ cup lemon juice and 1 teaspoon lemon zest. Cook in top of double boiler until thick. Remove from heat. Add butter or margarine and 2 stiffly beaten egg whites. Pour into baked pie shell.

Make meringue by beating remaining egg whites until stiff. Add remaining sugar, lemon zest, and lemon juice. Continue beating until meringue forms soft peaks. Spread over pie. Bake in a preheated 325-degree oven until meringue is browned, about 10 minutes. Serves six to eight.

PARADISE PECAN PRALINES

2 cups sugar
⅛ tsp. salt
¾ cup buttermilk
2 cups pecan halves

2 tbsp. butter
1 tsp. baking soda
½ tsp. vanilla extract

Combine all ingredients except baking soda and vanilla in an 8-cup glass measure. Microwave on 100 percent power for 12 minutes, stirring at 4-minute intervals. Stir in baking soda. Cook for 2 to 3 minutes on 100 percent power. Add vanilla; then beat mixture until glossy and drop by spoonful onto greased wax paper and allow to cool. Makes about three dozen.

PARISH PASTRY SHELL

1½ cups all-purpose flour
1 stick cold butter, cut into
  1-inch pieces

½ tsp. salt
3 to 4 tbsp. ice water

Insert metal blade in food processor. Add flour, butter, and salt. Process for 8 to 10 seconds, until mixture has the consistency of coarse meal. Pour ice water down feed tube and process dough, stopping just before it forms a ball. Take out of processor, wrap in plastic wrap or foil, and chill for 30 minutes to 1 hour. Roll dough out on a lightly floured board to ⅛-inch thickness. Fit into a 9-inch glass pie plate. Trim overhang to ½ inch. Fold overhang under and pinch to make decorative edge. Prick pastry with fork at ½-inch intervals. Makes one 9-inch pie shell.

MICROWAVE: Microwave pastry at 100 percent power for 4½ to 5 minutes or until pastry is opaque. Cool completely before filling.

CONVENTIONAL: Preheat oven to 425° F. Bake pastry for 12 to 15 minutes or until golden brown. Cool completely on wire rack before filling.

PETIT PECAN COOKIES

¼ lb. butter, softened
1 cup packed brown sugar
1 tsp. vanilla extract
1 egg

1 cup all-purpose flour
½ tsp. baking powder
1 cup pecans, coarsely
  chopped

In food processor fitted with metal blade, place pecans and pulse on and off until coarsely chopped. In a large bowl, cream butter and sugar. Add vanilla and egg, mixing well. In a medium bowl, sift flour with baking powder. Add gradually to butter mixture and stir in chopped pecans. Drop by rounded teaspoons onto ungreased cookie sheet. Bake in a preheated 350-degree oven for 12 to 15 minutes. Remove from sheet immediately and cool on rack. Makes three dozen.

PINKY'S CHOCOLATE PECAN PIE

4 1-oz. squares semisweet
  chocolate
3 tbsp. butter or margarine
1 tsp. instant coffee powder
3 eggs, slightly beaten
1 cup light corn syrup

⅓ cup sugar
1 tsp. vanilla extract
1 cup coarsely chopped
  pecans
1 unbaked 9-inch pastry
  shell

In a 1-quart saucepan, stir together chocolate, butter or margarine, and coffee powder. Stirring constantly, cook over low heat until chocolate is melted and mixture is smooth. In a medium bowl, stir together eggs, corn syrup, sugar, and vanilla until well blended. Stir in chocolate mixture and pecans; blend well. Pour mixture into pastry shell. Bake in a preheated 400-degree oven for 15 minutes. Reduce heat to 350° F. and bake an additional 50 to 55 minutes or until filling is set around edges. Cool on wire rack. Serves eight.

PRALINE POWDER

1½ cups granulated sugar
½ cup water

2 cups pecans

Combine sugar and water in a heavy saucepan. Place over medium heat. Add pecans. Cook, stirring with wooden spoon, until sugar dissolves and mixture becomes a light golden color. Remove from heat and pour onto a lightly oiled baking sheet.

When cold, break into 1-inch pieces. In food processor with metal blade in place, place candy pieces. Process, turning on and off, until evenly pulverized. Store in an airtight container in refrigerator until ready to use. Use in desserts, in sweet sauces, over ice cream, and in frostings and cake fillings. Makes about 3½ cups.

PURR-FEC PRALINES

1 cup brown sugar
1 cup granulated sugar
½ cup half-and-half

2 tbsp. butter
1 cup pecan halves

Dissolve sugars in half-and-half. Using a candy thermometer, heat to 228° F., stirring occasionally. Add butter and pecans. Cook until mixture reaches syrup stage or soft-ball stage (236° F.). Cool. Beat mixture until thick but still glossy. Drop by tablespoonfuls onto wax paper. Makes twelve.

RUM BREAD PUDDING

3 cups bread cubes
1½ cups evaporated milk
1 cup sugar
3 slightly beaten eggs
2 tsp. vanilla extract
¼ tsp. salt
1 tsp. cinnamon

½ cup raisins
1 large apple, peeled,
   cored, and sliced
¼ cup melted butter or
   margarine
Rum Sauce (see recipe)

In a 2-quart mixing bowl, combine bread cubes and evaporated milk. Let stand until bread absorbs milk (about 15 minutes). Stir in remaining ingredients and mix well. Pour into an 8-inch glass ring mold. Place on inverted microwave-safe plate. Microwave at 70 percent power for 15 minutes or until knife inserted near center comes out clean. Serves six.

RUM SAUCE

½ cup sugar
2 tbsp. cornstarch
¼ tsp. cinnamon
1 cup evaporated milk

½ cup milk
3 tbsp. butter or margarine
1 tbsp. rum

In a 2-quart glass measure, combine sugar, cornstarch, and cinnamon. Blend well. Stir in all milk. Microwave at 100 percent power for 2 minutes, stir well. Microwave at 100 percent power for 1 minute or until thick. Stir in margarine and rum. Stir well to blend. Spoon sauce over each serving. Serves six.

SHUK-A-LOT CAKE

½ cup vegetable shortening
1¼ cups sugar
3 eggs
2 2-oz. squares
  unsweetened chocolate,
  melted
1¾ cups all-purpose flour
1½ tsp. baking soda

¾ tsp. salt
¾ cup milk for microwave
  method or 1¼ cups milk
  for conventional method
1 tsp. vanilla
Chocolate Cream Frosting
  (see recipe)

MICROWAVE: Grease two 8-inch round glass cake dishes. Beat shortening and sugar together until light and fluffy. Add eggs one at a time, beating well after each addition. Beat in chocolate. Mix flour, baking soda, and salt. Add flour mixture alternately with milk to chocolate mixture, beating well after each addition. Stir in vanilla. Pour batter into prepared baking dishes. Microwave one layer at a time at 50 percent power for 5½ minutes, rotating once. Rotate layer again and microwave at 100 percent power for 1½ to 2 minutes or until center of layer is nearly dry. Place cake dish on heatproof surface. Cover tightly with plastic wrap and allow to cool for 10 minutes.

Remove cake by inverting pan and cool completely. Repeat with second layer. Fill and frost with Chocolate Cream Frosting. Makes one 8-inch 2-layer cake.

CONVENTIONAL: Grease two 8-inch round cake pans. Preheat oven to 350° F. Beat shortening and sugar together until light and fluffy. Add eggs one at a time, beating well after each addition. Beat in chocolate. Mix flour, baking soda, and salt. Add flour mixture alternately with milk to chocolate mixture, beating well after each addition. Stir in vanilla. Pour batter into prepared pans. Bake for 35 minutes or until cake tester inserted in center comes out clean. Cool in pans on wire rack for 10 minutes. Invert pans to remove cake layers and cool completely before filling and frosting with Chocolate Cream Frosting. Makes one 8-inch 2-layer cake.

CHOCOLATE CREAM FROSTING

½ cup butter
3 3-oz. squares
   unsweetened chocolate,
   melted (see note)
1 lb. confectioners' sugar
3 to 4 tbsp. half-and-half

½ tsp. vanilla extract
2 egg yolks
½ cup chopped pecans
pecan halves for
   decorations (optional)

Beat butter and chocolate in small mixer bowl until smooth and creamy. Gradually add sugar alternately with half-and-half. Beat in vanilla and egg yolks. If necessary, add more half-and-half to improve spreading consistency. Fold in chopped nuts. Spread frosting between layers, then frost top and sides of cake. Decorate top of cake with pecan halves, if desired.

NOTE: To melt chocolate in microwave oven, place unwrapped square in small glass bowl. Microwave at 50 percent power for 3 to 3½ minutes. Let stand for 2 to 3 minutes. Stir until smooth.

SUCRÉ ALMONDS

1 cup water
2 cups sugar
1 cup light corn syrup
1 lb. whole toasted
  blanched almonds

1 tsp. vanilla extract
2 cups coarse white or
  colored sugar

In a saucepan, bring water to a boil. Remove from heat and stir in sugar until thoroughly dissolved. Add corn syrup.

Over moderately high heat, cook until mixture reaches hard-ball stage (250° F. on candy thermometer). Remove from heat and quickly place pan in bowl of iced water to cool candy. Stir in nuts and vanilla. Remove nuts one by one from syrup and roll in coarse sugar. Place on rack covered with oiled parchment or wax paper to cool. Makes about 3½ cups.

SUPERPORT STRAWBERRY PIE

1 baked 9-inch pie shell
1½ qts. fresh strawberries
1 cup sugar

1 tsp. lemon juice
3 tbsp. cornstarch
½ cup water

Stem and rinse 2 cups strawberries. Place in a 1-quart microwave-safe casserole. Crush strawberries. Cook in microwave oven on 50 percent power for about 4 minutes or until berries are soft. Put cooked strawberries through a sieve to remove pulp and seeds. This should yield about 1½ cups juice (if necessary, add enough water to juice to make 1½ cups liquid). Add sugar, lemon juice, and cornstarch combined with water. Mix well. Cover with plastic wrap or microwave-safe cover. Cook on 50 percent power for 5 minutes or until mixture is thick and transparent, stirring 2 to 3 times during the last 2 minutes to avoid lumps. Cool glaze.

Stem and rinse remaining strawberries. If berries are large, slice them in half. Combine strawberries and cooled glaze. Spoon into baked pie shell. Garnish top with extra berries and whipped cream if desired. Cool and allow glaze to set before serving. Serves eight.

SYL'S STRAWBERRY PIE

1 9-inch baked pie shell
2 tbsp. sifted powdered
  sugar
1 qt. fresh strawberries

3 tbsp. cornstarch
3 tbsp. lemon juice
1 cup sugar
whipping cream (optional)

Sprinkle pie shell with powdered sugar and cover with half the berries. Crush remaining berries. Combine cornstarch, sugar, and lemon juice and mix with crushed berries. Cook over medium heat, stirring constantly, until mixture thickens and comes to a bubbling boil (about 10 minutes). Cool completely. Pour over berries in shell. Refrigerate for 1 to 2 hours. Pipe whipped cream on top before serving, if desired. Makes one 9-inch pie.

TRÈS BON CHERRIES JUBILEE

⅔ cup sugar
2 tbsp. cornstarch
⅛ tsp. salt
water
½ cup sweet red wine

1½ lbs. sweet bing
  cherries, pitted
⅓ cup cognac
1 qt. vanilla ice cream

MICROWAVE: Combine sugar, cornstarch, and salt in a 3-quart glass bowl or casserole. Stir in ½ cup water and wine until smooth. Add cherries and cover tightly with plastic wrap, turning back edge to vent. Microwave at 100 percent power for 8 to 9 minutes or until cherries are tender and sauce is thickened, stirring once. Meanwhile, scoop ice cream into dessert dishes. Place cognac in 1-cup glass measure. Microwave at 100 percent power for 30 to 40 seconds or until warm. Pour cherries into shallow serving dish. Pour warmed cognac gently and evenly over cherries. Ignite carefully with a long match. When flame goes out, ladle cherries over ice cream and serve immediately. Serves six to eight.

CONVENTIONAL: Combine sugar, cornstarch, and salt in a 3-quart saucepan. Stir in ¾ cup water and wine until smooth. Add cherries and heat to boiling. Reduce heat, cover, and simmer for 12 to 15 minutes or until cherries are tender and sauce is thickened, stirring occasionally. Meanwhile, scoop ice cream into dessert dishes. Pour cognac into small saucepan and place over low heat until just warm. Pour cherries into shallow serving dish. Pour warmed cognac gently and evenly over cherries. Ignite carefully with a long match. When flame goes out, ladle cherries over ice cream and serve immediately. Serves six to eight.

Purim in Israel

Let's take a detour to a part of the world where yet another group of settlers looking for freedom brought to a new land a potpourri of customs and ceremonies, a land where Kosher is King and the cuisine is as much a part of the culture as the cuisine of the Cajuns is of Louisiana. These are the settlers of Israel.

If you are fortunate enough to be touring Israel in early spring, you may join in the celebration of Purim there. Whether you are in the Negev in the southern part of Israel or in Tiberias in the Galilee in the north, or on a kibbutz in the east or a moshav in the west, or a small border settlement or the Holy City of Jerusalem, you will find that natives and tourists alike don costumes, wear masks, parade, and join in the general merriment of Purim. It is the only time in the Jewish year that one is actually enjoined to imbibe liberally of volatile liquid refreshments in order to increase the joy of the holiday. It is, in fact, obligatory and proper.

Purim is a fun holiday on which children and adults share the excitement and delight of reading the Megillah, the long story of the daring and beautiful Queen Esther, whose courage saved the Jewish people from annihilation. Haman, the arch villain, whose position today would be comparable to that of a prime minister, was determined to wipe out the Jewish people. Like the Acadians, the Persian Jews were persecuted, but unlike the Cajuns, the Jewish people had a hero, Mordecai, who through Esther was able to thwart Haman's plans.

Because Haman was hanged and Mordecai was rewarded, Jewish people throughout the world celebrate Purim. Every community has a carnival. The Jews of France introduced floats, riders, masquerades, and the carnival spirit to the Jewish world many centuries ago. And Israel introduced Adlayodah, the indoor carnival, throughout the diaspora. Both Cajun country and the Jewish world benefited from their "French connection"; the two cultures, so far apart, claim a common custom, the carnival.

Fun, food, and frivolity also bind both cultures. Cajuns celebrate every festival with food; likewise, the holiday of Purim commands an endless display of ethnic dishes and symbolic foods. As they say in every Jewish household, the Purim meal is a "Ganza Megillah" – it stretches from soup to Hamantaschen.

PURIM IN ISRAEL

CHICK PEA CROQUETTES

4 cups cooked chick peas
salt and pepper to taste
pinch marjoram
pinch thyme
¼ cup bread crumbs
4 eggs, beaten

4 tbsp. melted vegetable
  shortening
additional vegetable oil for
  frying
additional bread crumbs for
  rolling

Drain chick peas and place in food processor. With steel blade in place, pulse on and off 5 or 6 times or until puréed. Add seasonings to taste. Add bread crumbs, eggs, and melted shortening. Pulse once or twice until all ingredients are well mixed.

Remove mixture from food processor. Form into croquettes about 3 inches long and 1 inch in diameter. Roll in additional bread crumbs. Fry in deep hot fat until nicely brown. Drain on absorbent paper. Serve hot. Makes about three dozen.

FAIGEY'S FRUITED CHICKEN

2 tbsp. flour
½ tsp. salt
½ tsp. pepper
1 3- to 4-lb. fryer, cut into
  serving pieces
¼ cup peanut oil
½ cup dry white wine

⅓ cup orange juice
2 tbsp. honey
1 tbsp. chopped parsley
2 tbsp. slivered orange peel
1 cup halved seedless white
  grapes

Combine flour, salt and ¼ teaspoon pepper; use to dust chicken pieces lightly. In a big skillet, brown chicken in peanut oil. Add white wine, orange juice, honey, parsley, and remaining pepper. Cover; simmer over low heat for 30 minutes, stirring occasionally. Add orange peel.

Continue cooking until chicken is tender (10 to 15 minutes). Remove chicken to a warm serving platter. Add grapes to gravy and cook, stirring constantly, for 2 minutes. Pour over chicken. Garnish with additional grapes and orange slices, if desired. Serves four to five.

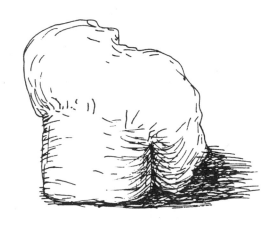

ESTHER'S LENTIL SOUP

1 cup dried lentils
1½ to 2 lbs. soup meat
1 onion
2 ribs celery, diced

1 carrot, diced
6 cups water
1 tbsp. salt
2 bay leaves

Soak lentils in enough cold water to cover for at least 2 hours. Drain. Add onion, celery, carrot, water, salt, and bay leaves. Cook in a covered pot for 1½ hours over moderate heat.

Strain vegetables and meat from soup. Set meat aside. Put vegetables in food processor with metal blade in place. Pulse on and off several times or until mixture is puréed. Return purée to strained liquid and stir in well. Heat through thoroughly. Serve soup meat on the side. Serves six.

DIRECTIONS FOR SHAPING
HAMANTASCHEN

To make a three-cornered fold, roll out dough ¼-inch thick. Cut into approximately 4-inch circles (or smaller for tea-size Hamantaschen). Put a teaspoon of filling in center of each circle and fold as shown in diagram below.

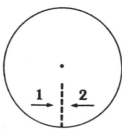

Pinch sides 1 and 2 together three-quarters of the way up the center, bringing the outsides together to form a V.

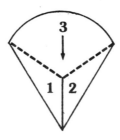

Bring top (3) down to meet 1 and 2.

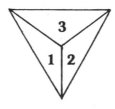

Pinch down 3 to complete the Hamantaschen three-cornered fold.

HAMANTASCHEN #1

½ cup sugar
¾ cup butter
1 tsp. grated lemon peel or
  ½ tsp. vanilla
2 eggs

2¼ cups flour
1 tsp. baking powder
Hamantaschen Filling (see
  recipes)

Mix sugar, butter, lemon peel or vanilla, and eggs in a medium bowl. Stir in flour and baking powder. If dough is too soft, stir in up to ¼ cup more flour. Cover and refrigerate until chilled, at least 1 hour.

Divide dough in half. Roll out each half ¼ inch thick on a lightly floured, cloth-covered board; cut into 3-inch circles.

Place a rounded teaspoonful filling on center of each circle. Place thumb, index finger, and middle fingers equal distances around edge of cookie; bring up sides of cookie. Pinch 3 corners together to form a triangle. Place cookies about 2 inches apart on an ungreased cookie sheet. Bake at 350° F. for 12 to 15 minutes. Immediately remove from cookie sheet; cool on rack. Makes about two dozen.

HAMANTASCHEN #2

6 cups flour
1 cake yeast
½ cup sugar
1 tbsp. salt
½ cup sour cream

1 pt. milk
½ cup butter
Hamantaschen Filling (see
  recipes)

Dissolve yeast in ¼ cup warm milk. Heat remaining milk and butter to lukewarm; beat. Add yeast mixture. Sift and add dry ingredients. Add sour cream and mix well. Knead at least 15 minutes; let rise in a warm place for 3 hours. Knead again for 15 minutes. Roll out dough ¼ inch thick. Cut into 4-inch circles.

Fill with filling, fold into 3-cornered shapes, and press edges together. Let rise until double in thickness. Bake 30 minutes in moderate oven (350° F.). Makes about twenty-four.

HUTZPAH HAMANTASCHEN

1 pkg. deluxe yellow cake
  mix (1 lb. 2.25 oz.
  package)
1 cup all-purpose flour

2 eggs
2 tbsp. water
Hamantaschen Filling (see
  recipes)

With electric mixer combine dry cake mix, flour, eggs, and water until well blended. Dough will be soft. Chill for 1 hour or more. On a lightly floured surface, roll out a quarter of the dough ⅛ inch thick. Cut into 2½- to 3-inch circles.

In center of each circle place 1 teaspoon filling. Bring edges together to form a triangle, pinching seams together from top down to corners, leaving a small opening in center. Repeat with remaining dough, working with a quarter of the dough at a time.

Place on a lightly greased cookie sheet. Bake at 375° F. for 6 minutes or until lightly browned. Remove and cool on rack. Makes about four dozen.

Hamantaschen Fillings

APRICOT-PECAN FILLING

½ cup dried apricots
½ cup firmly packed dark
  brown sugar

½ cup water
½ cup chopped pecans
1 tbsp. lemon juice

In a pan combine apricots with firmly packed dark brown sugar, water, chopped pecans, and lemon juice. Bring to a boil over medium heat, stirring constantly. Continue cooking, stirring occasionally, until mixture is thick, about 8 minutes. Cool. Makes filling for approximately four dozen Hamantaschen.

HONEY-NUT FILLING

**2 lbs. walnuts, finely
  chopped
1 pt. honey
½ tsp. cinnamon**

**grated rind of 1 lemon
½ tsp. vanilla extract**

Heat honey over medium flame. Add nuts, cinnamon, vanilla extract, and lemon rind. Bring to a boil. Lower flame and cook slowly for about 5 minutes. Cool. Makes filling for approximately four dozen Hamantaschen.

PRUNE FILLING

**1 cup mashed, cooked
  pitted prunes**

**3 tbsp. honey
2 tsp. lemon juice**

Mix together mashed fruit, honey, and lemon juice. Place a rounded teaspoonful filling on center of each Hamantaschen circle. Makes enough for two dozen Hamantaschen.

POPPY SEED FILLING

**1 cup poppy seeds
¼ cup chopped walnuts
1 tbsp. butter**

**1 tbsp. honey
1 tsp. lemon juice**

Mix together poppy seeds, walnuts, butter, honey, and lemon juice. Place a rounded teaspoonful on center of each Hamantaschen circle. Makes enough for two dozen Hamantaschen.

KAJUN KREPLACH

Thinly roll out basic noodle dough (see recipe below). Do not dry. Cut into 1½-inch squares. Place ½ teaspoon meat filling in center of squares and press edges together securely to form a triangle. Drop into boiling salted water. Cook, uncovered, for 10 to 15 minutes. When done, kreplach rise to the surface. Remove from pan and serve with soup or meat gravy. Makes about 2½ dozen.

BASIC NOODLE DOUGH

approximately 2 cups sifted flour

2 eggs
2 or 3 tsp. cold water

Place flour in mixing bowl or on kneading board. Make a well in center. Add eggs and combine with a fork, adding spoonfuls of water as necessary to form a ball of dough that is compact but not hard. Knead dough until as smooth and elastic as possible. Roll out on a lightly floured board. Use the rolling pin from the outer edges toward the center, turning the board as necessary in order to achieve easier rolling. Cut into 1½-inch squares for bite-size kreplach. Makes about 2½ dozen.

CHICKEN FILLING

1½ cups finely cut-up leftover cooked chicken
1 egg

1 tbsp. minced parsley
1 tsp. minced onion

Blend all ingredients together. Use ½ teaspoon filling for each bite-size kreplach. Makes enough for 2½ dozen kreplach.

KIBBUTZ KLUSTERS

1 egg
¾ cup firmly packed brown
  sugar
1¼ cups unsifted flour
½ tsp. baking soda

¼ tsp. salt
½ cup peanut oil
1 cup chopped unsalted
  peanuts
2 tsp. vanilla

Beat egg and blend in brown sugar. Combine flour, baking soda, and salt. Mix into egg and sugar mixture alternately with peanut oil. Stir in chopped peanuts and vanilla. Drop by teaspoonfuls onto lightly oiled baking sheets and bake in a moderate oven (375° F.) for 8 to 10 minutes or until done. Makes about 2½ dozen.

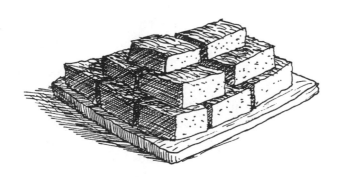

MORDECAI MUNCHÉES

⅓ cup shortening
1 cup brown sugar
1½ cups black molasses
½ cup cold water
7 cups sifted flour
1 tsp. salt

1 tsp. allspice
1 tsp. ginger
¼ tsp. cloves
¼ tsp. cinnamon
2 tsp. baking soda
3 tbsp. cold water

Frosting

1 cup confectioners' sugar
2 tbsp. water

few grains salt
½ tsp. vanilla

Decorations

slivered almonds
cinnamon drops for buttons

currants

Combine shortening with sugar and molasses, adding ½ cup cold water while stirring. Sift dry ingredients into a mixing bowl. Dissolve baking soda in 3 tablespoons cold water. Combine well, mixing all the above to form a ball of dough. Chill dough at least 1 hour in refrigerator.

Roll out dough on a lightly floured board or pat into a rectangle not more than ½ inch thick. Use a gingerbread man cutter to cut out figures. Roll dough remaining after cutting and pat out again or form little men by rolling small bits of dough in the palm of your hand and flattening as you form the figures on a well-greased cookie sheet. Arrange cut-out men and/or molded ones on a cookie sheet 1 inch apart. Bake for 18 to 20 minutes at 350° F.

Mix frosting to a consistency thin enough for spreading. When cookies are cold, decorate with frosting and press in slivered almonds over currants for eyes. Use red cinnamon candies for shoe and coat buttons, with or without slivered almonds. If desired, use points of Brazil nuts for shoes. Makes 1 dozen large cookies.

NAHIT À LA NEGEV

1 lb. nahit peas
1 tbsp. salt
¼ tsp. baking soda
2 tbsp. chicken fat

2 tbsp. flour
2 tbsp. sugar
½ lb. brisket of beef
hot water as needed

Place peas in a kettle, add salt and hot water to cover, and let soak for 12 hours. Drain and reserve 1 cup liquid. Return peas to kettle, cover with boiling water, and cook for 15 minutes. Add soda and meat and let cook slowly until peas are tender.

Melt chicken fat, add flour and sugar, and let brown. Add reserved liquid from peas; cook until thick and smooth. Pour over peas and meat and cook thoroughly. Place in a casserole and bake in a moderate oven (350° F.) for 30 minutes. Serves four to six.

NATCH'ULLY NAHIT

1 lb. dry chick peas

salt to taste

Soak chick peas in enough cold water to cover for 10 to 12 hours. Drain and rinse in cold water. Add fresh water to come 2 inches over top of peas. Cook in a covered pot for 30 to 40 minutes, add salt to taste, and continue cooking uncovered till tender. Drain, dust lightly with salt, and serve hot or cold.

PERSIAN PURIM PEAS

1 cup cooked nahit
¼ cup raw rice
3 cups water

1 tsp. salt
½ cup honey
¼ cup brown sugar

Combine all ingredients and cook over moderate heat for 20 to 30 minutes or until rice is tender. Turn into a casserole. Bake at 400° F. for 15 minutes or until nicely browned on top. Serves four to five.

POPPY SEED CHEESECAKE

butter or margarine
¼ cup ground macaroons
1¼ cups sugar
3 tbsp. flour
1 2-oz. pkg. poppy seeds
2 8-oz. pkgs. cream cheese
6 eggs, separated

1 tsp. vanilla
½ tsp. almond extract
grated peel of 1 orange
1 cup sour cream
dash salt
½ tsp. cream of tartar
powdered sugar

Butter a 9-inch springform pan and sprinkle with ground macaroons. Set aside.

Combine ¾ cup sugar, flour, and poppy seeds in large bowl of electric mixer. Add cream cheese and beat until smooth and fluffy. Beat in egg yolks, one at a time, blending well after each addition. Add vanilla, almond extract, orange peel, and sour cream. Blend well.

Beat egg whites until foamy. Add salt and cream of tartar and beat until stiff peaks form. Gradually add remaining sugar and beat until stiff. Fold into cream cheese mixture.

Pour into prepared springform pan. Place pan of water on lower rack of oven. Place cheesecake on center rack. Bake at 325° F. for 1½ hours or until cake is firm in center. Turn off heat and let cool in oven for 1 hour. Remove from oven.

Loosen cake from sides of pan with spatula, but do not remove until ready to serve. Just before serving, sprinkle with powdered sugar. Serves ten to twelve.

SHUSHAN PURIM STEW

½ cup unsifted flour
5 tsp. salt
1⅛ tsp. pepper
2½ lbs. round or chuck
  beef, cut into cubes
¼ cup peanut oil
1 cup water
1 tbsp. chopped parsley

2 tsp. minced garlic
½ bay leaf, crumbled
1 tsp. rosemary leaves
½ lb. fresh mushrooms,
  sliced
2 cups thinly sliced onions
1 cup sliced green pepper
hot cooked noodles

Combine flour, ½ teaspoon salt and ⅛ teaspoon pepper. Dredge beef cubes in flour mixture. Heat peanut oil in a Dutch oven and brown beef cubes. Add water, remaining salt, parsley, garlic, bay leaf, rosemary leaves, and remaining pepper. Cover and simmer for about 1½ hours or until meat is tender. Stir occasionally. Add mushrooms, sliced onions, and green pepper.

Cook for an additional 10 minutes. If gravy is too thin, sprinkle 1 tablespoon flour over ragout and blend thoroughly. Serve over noodles. Serves six to eight.

Crowley
RICE

Along the bayous of Acadia Parish lie 400,000 acres of fertile land that nature seems to have designed especially for growing rice. It has made Acadia Parish the undisputed queen of all the rice country. In the midst of this agricultural empire is the bustling town of Crowley, the "Rice City of America."

This beautiful land lay dormant until the settling of the Evangeline people. Seeking new homelands after their cruel exile from Nova Scotia, the Evangelines were the first to bring this soil under the magic of their plow. Soon after landing in St. Martinville in 1757, some of the more daring settlers ventured into what were then Indian hunting grounds. They discovered the fertility of the lands along the bayou and built homes there. To this day their descendants comprise the larger part of the population of Crowley.

The history of Crowley unfolds as a tour of the town reveals the role this community plays in the world's rice production. Crowley's first rice mill was built by Squire Pickett, and the first rice was milled there in 1893 in a two-story structure with machinery operated by a fifty-horsepower engine, a far cry from the modern mills seen in Crowley today. The first mill did much to center the rice industry and give Crowley the distinction of being "the rice city of America."

On highway U.S. 90 West in Crowley is a Rice Museum containing exhibits about the rice industry, along with artifacts and memorabilia of Acadian culture and a history of the town. Another landmark is the Rice Experiment Station, a research organization of the rice industry which was established in Crowley in 1909. October is an excellent time to plan your tour of this part of Cajun country, when the International Rice Festival is held. This festival, like all Cajun festivals, gives visitors a chance to taste a variety of regional dishes. Rice has always been the staple of Cajun cooking, and nowhere in the world is the preparation of rice taken as seriously as in the Cajun kitchen.

From a barren prairie selling for fifty cents an acre in 1886, Crowley has changed to a thriving, up-to-date little city, offering every inducement and the best of opportunities to the investor, the manufacturer, the merchant, the professional, and the working man. The citizens of Crowley, their Cajun charm intact, are often heard to say, "le bon changement." It has indeed been "a good change."

RICE

Celestine's Cajun Dressing *(Microwave)*
Crowley Crepes *(Processor and Conventional)*
Rice Filling *(Conventional)*
Sour Cream Sauce *(Conventional)*
Davener's Dirty Rice *(Conventional)*
Fry-Mi-Fritters *(Conventional)*
Kinsmen Casserole *(Microwave)*
Kosher-Cajun Rice Dressing *(Conventional)*
Mae Belle's Meatballs on Rice *(Microwave)*
Pepy's Pecan Rice *(Conventional)*
Reece's Rice and Broccoli *(Conventional)*
Rice Beignets *(Conventional)*
Rice City Pudding *(Microwave and Conventional)*
Rice-o-Razel *(Conventional)*
Rice: The Easy Way *(Microwave)*
Ring-Around-Rice *(Conventional)*
Rowena's Rice Pie *(Conventional)*
Sham and Egg Jambalaya *(Microwave)*
Squashées *(Conventional)*
Squire's Jambalaya Salad *(Processor and Conventional)*
Tante's Tuna and Rice *(Processor and Microwave)*
Tzicken Mit Rice *(Microwave)*

CELESTINE'S CAJUN DRESSING

1 lb. ground beef
1 lb. chicken gizzards,
  ground
¼ cup pareve margarine
2 cups chopped onions
1 cup chopped celery
2 cloves garlic, chopped
1 10-oz. can kosher
  condensed chicken soup
1 tbsp. Worcestershire
  sauce

½ tsp. garlic salt
½ tsp. ground white pepper
½ tsp. cayenne pepper
½ tsp. black pepper
¼ tsp. dry mustard
¼ tsp. crushed basil
½ cup chopped shallots
½ cup chopped parsley
2 tbsp. pareve margarine
6 cups cooked rice

In 5-quart microwave-safe casserole, combine ground beef and gizzards. Mix well. Microwave on High (100 percent power) for 6 to 8 minutes or until meat is no longer pink, stirring halfway through cooking time. In a 1-quart glass measure, combine ¼ cup pareve margarine, onions, celery, and garlic. Microwave on High for 4 to 5 minutes or until soft but not brown. Add sautéed vegetables to meat mixture. Add chicken soup, Worcestershire sauce, salt, peppers, mustard, and basil. Cover with plastic wrap. Microwave on High for 5 minutes. Stir. Microwave on Medium (50 percent power) for additional 20 to 25 minutes or until hot and well seasoned. In a 4-cup glass measure, combine shallots, parsley, and 2 tablespoons pareve margarine. Microwave on High for 2 to 3 minutes or until soft. Add shallots and rice to meat mixture, mix well, and serve. Serves twelve.

CROWLEY CREPES

1 tbsp. cooked rice
1¼ cups all-purpose flour
1½ cups milk
2 eggs
2 tbsp. sour cream

⅛ tsp. salt
Rice Filling (see recipe)
Sour Cream Sauce (see
  recipe)

In food processor fitted with metal blade, mix rice, flour, milk, eggs, sour cream, and salt for 30 seconds. Pour batter into a bowl and refrigerate for about 2 hours.

To prepare crepes, pour 3 tablespoons of batter into a greased and heated crepe pan or small skillet. Cook until done on one side. Crepes do not need to be cooked on both sides. Remove crepe from pan and place a small amount of Rice Filling on each crepe. Fold crepe around the filling. Serve with Sour Cream Sauce on top of each crepe. Makes about twelve.

RICE FILLING

1 cup cooked rice
1/3 cup chopped onions
1/3 cup chopped pickles
1 hard-cooked egg,
   chopped

1 tbsp. lemon juice
2 tbsp. mayonnaise
salt and pepper to taste

Mix all ingredients in a large bowl. Place about 1 tablespoon filling in each crepe. Makes enough filling for about twelve crepes.

SOUR CREAM SAUCE

8 oz. sour cream
4 tbsp. vinegar

2 tsp. sugar
1/2 tsp. salt

Beat all ingredients until smooth and creamy. Refrigerate until ready to serve. Spoon over crepes. Makes enough sauce for about twelve crepes.

DAVENER'S DIRTY RICE

2 medium onions, chopped
2 ribs celery, chopped
4 shallots, chopped
3 tbsp. vegetable oil
¼ lb. chicken gizzards, chopped
½ lb. ground beef
2 tbsp. chopped parsley
¼ lb. broiled kosher chicken livers, chopped

1 kosher beef bouillon cube
½ cup hot water
1 tbsp. Worcestershire sauce
salt, cayenne pepper, and black pepper to taste
3 cups cooked white rice

Sauté onions, celery, and shallots in vegetable oil until soft, about 10 minutes. Add gizzards, ground beef, and parsley.

Brown meats thoroughly. Add chicken livers. Dissolve beef bouillon cube in water and add to meat mixture, together with seasonings and Worcestershire sauce. Cover and simmer over low heat for 30 minutes. Remove from heat, add to cooked rice, and mix well. Serves eight.

FRY-MI-FRITTERS

2 cups mashed, cooked eggplant
1½ cups cooked rice
2 tsp. grated onion
2 eggs, slightly beaten
1 cup grated sharp cheddar cheese

¼ cup all-purpose flour
1½ tsp. salt
½ tsp. pepper
dash Tabasco sauce
vegetable oil for frying (enough to measure ½ inch deep in frying pan)

Combine eggplant with remaining ingredients except oil. Mix well. Heat oil to deep-frying temperature (350° F. on cooking thermometer). Drop rice mixture from spoon into hot oil. Fry until browned on each side. Makes twelve.

KINSMEN CASSEROLE

1 10-oz. pkg. frozen
   broccoli
3 eggs
1 13-oz. can evaporated
   milk
⅔ cup quick-cooking rice,
   uncooked

½ lb. kosher American
   cheese, cut into cubes
½ tsp. salt
¼ tsp. cayenne pepper
¼ cup chopped onion

Microwave broccoli in a 1-quart casserole on High for 5 to 6 minutes. Drain well and set aside. Mix eggs, evaporated milk, rice, cheese, salt, and cayenne pepper in a 2-quart casserole. Microwave on High for 5 to 6 minutes, stirring after 2 minutes until cheese melts.

Add onion and broccoli to rice mixture and pour into a 10-inch × 6-inch × 2-inch baking dish. Microwave on High for 10 to 12 minutes or until center is set. Serves six to eight.

KOSHER-CAJUN RICE DRESSING

3 cups cooked white rice
1½ lbs. ground beef
½ cup chopped onions
¾ cup chopped celery,
   including some leaves
salt and pepper to taste

¼ tsp. dried thyme
1 cup kosher canned
   condensed chicken soup
1 cup sliced shallots
½ cup chopped parsley

In a large pot, cook ground beef with onions and celery, stirring often. Add salt and pepper to taste. When meat begins to sizzle and brown, add thyme and chicken soup. Cover and simmer for 20 minutes or until almost all liquid has evaporated. Remove from heat; stir in shallots and parsley. Add cooked rice. Stir until well mixed. Bake, covered, for 20 minutes at 350° F. Serve in casserole or as stuffing for fowl. Serves eight.

MAE BELLE'S MEATBALLS
ON RICE

1 lb. ground beef	2 cups sliced fresh
¾ cup chopped onion	mushrooms
¼ cup bread crumbs	½ cup chopped celery
1 egg	2 cups quick-cooking rice
3 tbsp. Worcestershire	1 10-oz. can kosher pareve
sauce	mushroom soup
1 tsp. salt	1 cup water
¼ tsp. cayenne pepper	

Combine ground beef, ¼ cup onion, bread crumbs, egg, 1 table-spoon Worcestershire sauce, salt, and cayenne pepper. Shape into 20 to 25 small meatballs.

Place in a 12-inch × 8-inch microwave-safe baking dish. Microwave on High for 5 to 6 minutes or until set but meat is still slightly pink. Rearrange and turn after half the cooking time. Drain meatballs on paper towels. Add remaining onion, mushrooms, and celery to dish. Cover with plastic wrap. Microwave on High for 4 to 7 minutes or until tender. Drain all but 2 tablespoons fat from dish.

Mix in remaining Worcestershire sauce, rice, mushroom soup, and water. Arrange meatballs on top. Cover. Microwave on High for 5 to 7 minutes or until rice is tender and liquid is absorbed, pushing rice at edge of dish toward center after half the cooking time. Serves four.

PEPY'S PECAN RICE

½ cup pecan pieces	¼ cup chopped parsley
¼ cup butter or pareve	2 cups cooked rice
margarine	

Brown pecan pieces in butter or pareve margarine. Add parsley. Mix into 2 cups hot cooked rice and serve. Serves four to six.

REECE'S RICE AND BROCCOLI

½ stick butter
1 onion, chopped
1 rib celery, chopped
1 10-oz. pkg. broccoli,
  chopped
1 cup cooked rice

1 10-oz. can kosher cream
  of mushroom soup
¼ lb. grated cheddar
  cheese
⅛ tsp. Tabasco sauce
pepper to taste

In a skillet sauté onions and celery in butter. Add broccoli, rice, soup, and cheese. Season to taste with Tabasco and pepper. Pour in a greased 1½-quart casserole dish. Bake at 350° F. for 30 to 40 minutes. Serves four.

RICE BEIGNETS

1 cup uncooked rice
6 oz. kosher salami,
  coarsely chopped
2 eggs, separated

½ cup tomato sauce
½ cup kosher seasoned
  bread crumbs
vegetable oil for frying

Cook rice. Fold into rice, salami, egg yolks, and tomato sauce. Shape into 12 balls. Beat egg whites lightly in shallow dish. Place bread crumbs in another shallow pan. Gently roll rice balls in egg whites, then dip in bread crumbs to coat evenly. Chill several hours or until balls are firm.

In a deep frying pan heat about 3 inches of oil to 375° F. Fry rice balls a few at a time, turning once, until nicely brown, about 4 minutes. Drain on absorbent towels. Serves six.

RICE CITY PUDDING

4 cups milk
⅔ cup long-grain rice
½ cup sugar
½ cup dark seedless raisins
1 tbsp. grated orange zest
½ tsp. vanilla extract

¼ tsp. cinnamon
¼ tsp. salt
2 eggs, well beaten
¾ cup water (for
   conventional recipe only)

MICROWAVE: Combine milk and rice in a 2-quart casserole. Cover tightly with plastic wrap, turning back edge to vent. Microwave on 100 percent power for 7 minutes, stirring once. Stir in sugar, raisins, orange zest, vanilla extract, cinnamon, and salt. Cover, leaving vent, and microwave at 50 percent power for 30 minutes, stirring twice. Beat a little hot rice mixture into eggs. Pour egg mixture into casserole and blend. Microwave on 50 percent power for 3 minutes or until set, rotating casserole once. Serves six.

CONVENTIONAL: Grease a 2-quart casserole dish. Preheat oven to 325° F. In a saucepan, heat rice and ¾ cup water to boiling. Reduce heat, cover, and simmer for 10 minutes. Gradually add milk and sugar. Heat until tiny bubbles form around edge of saucepan. Stir in raisins, orange zest, vanilla, cinnamon, and salt. Place beaten eggs in casserole and gradually beat in hot milk mixture. Place casserole in a large baking dish and add boiling water to come halfway up side of casserole. Bake 1 hour and 15 minutes or until knife inserted in center comes out clean. Serves six.

RICE-O-RAZEL

1 12-oz. pkg. kosher
  smoked sausages
2 cups raw rice
2 kosher beef bouillon
  cubes
2 cups hot water
¼ lb. pareve margarine

4 tbsp. chopped celery
4 tbsp. chopped parsley
4 tbsp. chopped shallots
4 tbsp. chopped bell pepper
1 cup water
1 tsp. Worcestershire sauce

Rinse rice. Slice sausages in half and brown in a large, heavy oven-proof skillet. Dissolve bouillon cubes in hot water. Add rice, bouillon, and all other ingredients to skillet. Mix well. Place skillet in oven and bake uncovered at 350° F. until liquid is absorbed, about 30 minutes. Stir and cover; then place skillet on top of stove and cook an additional 5 to 10 minutes, stirring occasionally. Serves six.

RICE: THE EASY WAY

2 cups water
1 tsp. salt

1 tbsp. pareve margarine
1 cup long-grain white rice

In a 2-quart microwave-safe bowl, combine water, salt, and margarine. Cover with plastic wrap. Microwave on 100 percent power for 5 to 6 minutes or until boiling. Stir in rice. Cover with plastic wrap. Microwave on low (30 percent power) for 16 to 18 minutes, or until most of the liquid is absorbed by rice. Let stand, covered, 5 minutes before serving. Serves four to six.

RING-AROUND-RICE

6 cups hot cooked rice
3 10-oz. pkgs. frozen
   chopped spinach
1 tbsp. pareve margarine

1 clove garlic, minced
1 small onion, finely
   chopped
3 16-oz. cans corn

Cook spinach according to package directions. Melt margarine in skillet. Sauté garlic and onion until wilted and translucent. Break up cooked spinach. Combine spinach, onion, garlic, and rice and press into a heated 2½-quart ring mold. Turn out on a hot platter. Fill center with hot corn. Serves ten to twelve.

ROWENA'S RICE PIE

2 10-oz. pkgs. frozen
   spinach
5 tbsp. vegetable oil
1 clove garlic, crushed
1 medium onion, finely
   chopped
⅛ tsp. cayenne pepper
salt and additional pepper
   to taste

4 eggs
¼ cup milk
5 tbsp. grated Parmesan
   cheese
8 oz. mozzarella cheese,
   grated
1 cup cooked rice

Cook spinach for 5 minutes, according to package directions, and squeeze dry. In a pan, heat oil and sauté garlic and onion. Add cayenne, salt, and additional pepper to taste.

Mix together spinach, eggs, Parmesan, milk, and half of the mozzarella cheese. Add onion mixture and cooked rice, mixing well.

Grease a 10-inch pie pan and fill with spinach-rice mixture. Bake in a 375-degree oven for 20 minutes or until lightly browned. Sprinkle the remaining mozzarella cheese over pie and continue baking for 10 minutes more. Serves six to eight.

SHAM AND EGG JAMBALAYA

4 tbsp. pareve margarine
½ cup chopped onions
¼ lb. kosher pastrami, cut
   into pieces

2 cups cooked rice
4 eggs, beaten
½ tsp. salt
¼ tsp. pepper

In a 2-quart microwave-safe casserole, combine pareve margarine, onions, and pastrami. Microwave on High (100 percent power) for 3 to 4 minutes or until onions are soft but not brown. Add rice, eggs, salt, and pepper. Mix well. Cover with plastic wrap. Microwave on Medium-High (70 percent power) for 5 to 7 minutes or until hot and eggs are set. Let stand, covered, for 2 minutes before serving. Serves four.

SQUASHÉES

4 medium butternut squash
⅔ cup packed brown sugar
⅔ cup white sugar
⅛ tsp. ground nutmeg
¼ tsp. salt

4 tsp. lemon juice
5 tbsp. butter or pareve
   margarine
1 cup pecans, chopped
1 cup cooked rice

Scrub skin of squash. Cut squash in half and remove seedy part. Place squash, meaty side down, in about an inch of water in a large baking pan. Bake in a 350-degree oven about 30 minutes or until tender. Remove from pan and cool.

When cool, remove squash meat from shells. Set shells aside. Mash squash well and add brown sugar, white sugar, nutmeg, salt, lemon juice, butter or pareve margarine, pecans, and rice. Place mixture in squash shells. Bake in a 350-degree oven until brown, about 30 minutes. Serves eight.

SQUIRE'S JAMBALAYA SALAD

1 large egg plus 2 egg yolks
⅓ cup tarragon vinegar
3 tbsp. whole-grain
   mustard
1½ tsp. salt
2 tsp. black pepper
2¼ cups olive oil
1 medium onion, finely
   chopped
⅛ tsp. cayenne pepper
½ tsp. crushed thyme
2 bay leaves
2 cups kosher condensed
   chicken soup
1 cup raw long-grain white
   rice
3 ribs celery, cut diagonally
   into ½-inch pieces

1 small green bell pepper,
   cut into 1-inch pieces
1 small red bell pepper, cut
   into 1-inch pieces
4 shallots, thinly sliced
1½ cups diced cooked
   chicken
1½ cups (about ¾ lb.)
   diced kosher salami
1 large head of lettuce,
   coarsely shredded
2 ripe tomatoes, each cut
   into 6 wedges, or 12
   cherry tomatoes
3 hard-cooked eggs, cut
   into quarters

In food processor fitted with metal blade, combine whole egg, egg yolks, vinegar, mustard, ½ teaspoon of salt and black pepper. Process for 1 minute. With machine on, pour in 2 cups olive oil in a steady stream. Remove from processor, cover, and refrigerate until serving time.

In a medium saucepan, heat 3 tablespoons olive oil. Add chopped onion and sauté, stirring, over moderate heat until limp and tender, about 5 minutes. Add cayenne pepper, thyme, and bay leaves and cook, stirring, for 2 to 3 minutes. Stir in chicken soup, remaining salt and rice. Increase heat to moderate-high and bring mixture to a boil. Reduce heat to low, cover pan, and cook for 20 minutes or until rice is tender and all liquid is absorbed. Remove from heat and let stand, covered, for 5 minutes. Scrape rice into a large bowl, remove bay leaves, and let stand, stirring occasionally, until cool.

Add celery, green and red bell peppers, shallots, chicken, salami, and remaining tablespoon olive oil. Toss well to mix.

To serve, line 6 large plates with shredded lettuce. Place about 1½ cups of rice salad in center of plate. Garnish each plate with 2 tomato wedges or 2 cherry tomatoes, and 2 hard-cooked egg quarters. Drizzle with dressing. Serves six.

TANTE'S TUNA AND RICE

1 green pepper, chopped
1 small onion, chopped
6 tbsp. pareve margarine
¼ cup flour
½ cup nondairy creamer
½ cup water
2 cups quick-cooking rice
2 6½-oz. cans tuna fish
1 10-oz. can kosher condensed chicken soup
1 10-oz. can kosher pareve mushroom soup
1 2-oz. jar pimentos
1 4-oz. can mushrooms, drained
salt and pepper to taste

In food processor fitted with steel blade, process green pepper and onion until coarsely chopped.

In a 10-inch glass microwave-safe dish, sauté onion and green pepper in pareve margarine for 5 minutes at 50 percent power. Blend in flour and add nondairy creamer and water. Stir until smooth. Return to microwave and cook at 50 percent power for 2 minutes, stirring twice. Add rice to sauce and mix until completely coated. Mix in remaining ingredients, seasoning to taste. Cook on 50 percent power for 10 minutes, turning every 2½ minutes. Serves eight.

TZICKEN MIT RICE

1 10-oz. can kosher
   condensed chicken soup
2 cups raw quick-cooking
   rice
½ cup water
1 4-oz. can mushroom
   pieces, drained

1 2-oz. envelope kosher dry
   onion soup mix
2- to 3-lb. fryer chicken
   pieces

Combine all ingredients except chicken in a 12-inch × 8-inch microwave-safe dish. Arrange chicken pieces on top, bony side up and meatier pieces to outside of dish. Cover with plastic wrap. Microwave on 100 percent power for 5 minutes. Reduce power to 50 percent. Microwave for 15 minutes. Turn chicken over and rearrange so the least cooked portions are to the outside of the dish. Microwave for 20 minutes on 50 percent power or until chicken is tender and no longer pink near the bone. Serves six.

Lake Charles

VEGETABLES

"Gumbeaux Gator," the seven-foot alligator, is Lake Charles and southwest Louisiana's ambassador of goodwill. He extends a warm "bonjour" to the Cajun Fun Country. The language, architecture, ways of relaxation, and especially the food in the area have all been influenced by the Cajun heritage. Everyone here feels a Cajun connection.

Lake Charles, the hub of this part of the country, is a city with an exciting past and an equally exciting future. The French settled here in the 1760s. Charles and Catherine Sallier built the first home on the lake's edge, prompting others to refer to the town as "Charlie's Lake" and then later as Lake Charles.

Jean Lafitte had his headquarters in and around Lake Charles. The legendary pirate and his privateers regularly robbed the Spanish ships on the high seas; according to legend, this is where he hid his contraband, and supposedly it remains hidden here to this day. "Contraband Days" is a thirteen-day celebration held here in the spring. Jean Lafitte springs to life as the "gentleman pirate" sails along the shores with Miss Contraband at his side. His buccaneers parade at night, and the lake becomes the center of an endless stream of activities.

Lake Charles continues to maintain its own distinct Cajun history and culture, from the "Cajun Riviera" to the Charpentier District. Along the "Riviera's" beaches, fun-loving natives and visitors alike can enjoy the white sands of North Beach and drink in the sun during warm weather. The Charpentier District is a twenty-block area in downtown Lake Charles where Victorian homes were built at the turn of the century by area carpenters using a variety of architecture patterns. The carpenters would combine styles to suit the taste and need of each homeowner. Authorities on Victorian architecture refer to it as "Lake Charles-style architecture."

With nearly 80,000 people of various backgrounds, Lake Charles has maintained the unique distinction of being the best of Louisiana's "Sportsman's Paradise" with turn-of-the-century Victorian charm. It is also an attractive, modern city with international commerce, a very busy deep-water port, oil and gas reserves, and a large, spread-out petro-chemical complex.

Lake Charles epitomizes the ABC of Cajun Fun Country: Architecture, Beaches, and Cajun Cuisine. And as Gumbeaux the Gator welcomes you with his "bonjour," he is likely to add "c'est bon," for it is all good in Lake Charles.

VEGETABLES

Artichoke à la Amanda *(Processor and Conventional)*
Broccoli by Beulah *(Processor)*
Casserole de Jean *(Microwave)*
Cauli's Flower *(Conventional)*
Coonie's Compote *(Conventional)*
Cora's Corn Pudding *(Conventional)*
Country Corn *(Microwave)*
Crab-Corn *(Conventional)*
Eggplant en Casserole *(Conventional)*
Eppes Essen Eggplant *(Microwave and Conventional)*
Gator Green Beans *(Microwave and Conventional)*
Lake Charles Okra Fritters *(Processor and Conventional)*
Okra Corn-nelia *(Processor and Conventional)*
Okra "Jambeaux" *(Processor and Conventional)*
Ora Mae's Baked Onions *(Conventional)*
Paradise Potatoes *(Microwave and Conventional)*
Paw-Paw's Stuffed Potatoes *(Conventional)*
Red Beans Cajun-Style I *(Microwave and Processor)*
Red Beans Cajun-Style II *(Processor and Conventional)*
Su-Sue's Spinach *(Conventional)*
Vegetables C'est Bon *(Microwave)*

ARTICHOKE À LA AMANDA

1 medium onion
1 large rib celery
1 small bell pepper
4 tbsp. butter or margarine
3 14-oz. cans artichoke
   hearts

½ cup grated Parmesan
   cheese
1 tbsp. olive oil
½ cup kosher seasoned
   bread crumbs
2 tbsp. imitation bacon bits

In a food processor fitted with metal blade, process onion, celery, and bell pepper until chopped fine. Remove and sauté in melted butter or margarine until tender.

Drain artichoke hearts and cut into quarters. Combine with softened vegetables. Add cheese, olive oil, and bread crumbs. Mix well. Place in a 1½-quart casserole dish and top with additional bread crumbs if desired. Bake uncovered at 325° F. for 20 to 30 minutes. Sprinkle imitation bacon bits on top before serving. Serves six.

BROCCOLI BY BEULAH

2 bunches fresh broccoli (1
   to 1½ lbs. each)
1½ cups water
1½ tsp. salt
⅓ cup clear kosher chicken
   broth

2 tsp. lemon juice
dash oregano
dash rosemary
3 eggs

Trim off and discard broccoli leaves and ends of stems. Separate into spears. In saucepan bring water to a boil. Add 1 teaspoon salt and broccoli. Cover and cook 10 to 12 minutes, until tender. Drain and cool slightly. Reserve about 8 small florets for garnish.

Preheat oven to 325° F. Spray eight 5-ounce custard cups with nonstick vegetable spray. Arrange cups in shallow baking pan.

In food processor fitted with steel blade, combine cooked broccoli, chicken broth, lemon juice, remaining salt, oregano, and rosemary.

Process until almost smooth, scraping bowl once or twice. Add eggs. Process just until well mixed. Spoon into prepared custard cups.

Pour ½ inch boiling water into pan. Place in oven. Bake 40 to 45 minutes or until knife inserted near center of cup comes out clean. Let stand 5 minutes. To unmold run tip of knife around edge of cups, then invert onto serving platter. Garnish with reserved florets. Serves eight.

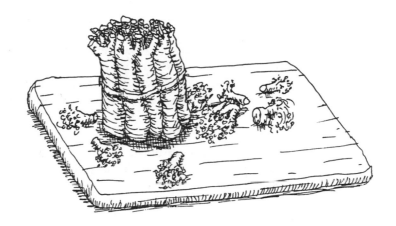

CASSEROLE DE JEAN

⅓ cup butter
2 medium onions, sliced
1 eggplant, cut into ½-inch cubes (about 1½ lbs.)
1 tsp. salt

3 medium tomatoes, cut into wedges or sliced
1 cup shredded American cheese

Melt butter in a 2½-quart casserole dish. Add onion and eggplant. Cover and microwave on 50 percent power for 7 minutes, stirring twice. Mix in salt. Arrange tomato slices or wedges on top. Sprinkle with shredded cheese. Continue to cook on 50 percent power for 10 to 12 minutes or until cheese bubbles, turning casserole after the first 5 minutes. Serves four to six.

CAULI'S FLOWER

1 large head cauliflower
1 large bunch broccoli
4 to 6 tbsp. olive oil
3 cloves garlic, chopped
½ cup kosher condensed
   chicken soup, undiluted

salt and pepper to taste
juice of 1 lemon
½ tsp. finely grated lemon
   zest

Separate cauliflower into florets. Trim tough stems from broccoli and discard. Slice remaining stems into thin rounds. Break florets into small pieces. Rinse vegetables under cold water and drain thoroughly.

Heat oil in a large skillet over medium heat. Add garlic and cook until golden in color; do not overcook. Remove garlic with slotted spoon and set aside.

Increase heat to high. Add cauliflower and broccoli and cook for 2 minutes, stirring occasionally. Add chicken soup and mix well. Cover and cook until vegetables are crisp-tender, about 2 or 3 minutes, adding a small amount of liquid if needed to prevent burning.

Remove cover and continue cooking about 1 more minute to evaporate remaining liquid. Add salt and pepper to taste. Mix in garlic and lemon juice. Serve in preheated serving dish. Sprinkle with lemon zest. Serves eight to ten.

COONIE'S COMPOTE

4 strips Beef Frye
½ cup sugar
1 tbsp. cornstarch
1 tsp. salt
¼ tsp. pepper
⅔ cup white vinegar
1 medium onion, sliced

1 16-oz. can green lima
  beans, drained
1 16-oz. can large butter
  beans, drained
1 15-oz. can red kidney
  beans, drained

In a large saucepan or frying pan, fry Beef Frye until crisp. Remove and drain on paper towels. To drippings add sugar and cornstarch; blend well. Stir in salt, pepper, and vinegar. Heat until mixture boils and thickens. Stir in onion and drained beans. Cover and simmer over low heat for 20 to 25 minutes, stirring occasionally. Crumble Beef Frye and sprinkle over top before serving. Serves eight.

CORA'S CORN PUDDING

3 cups fresh corn kernels
  (about 6 medium ears)
3 large eggs
3 tbsp. flour
1½ tsp. salt
1½ tsp. sugar
¾ tsp. baking powder

¼ tsp. cayenne pepper
3 tbsp. melted butter or
  pareve margarine
1 cup milk or ½ cup water
  and ½ cup nondairy
  creamer combined

Preheat oven to 350° F.
In a small bowl, beat eggs lightly. Add corn and all remaining ingredients. Mix well. Place corn mixture in a greased 1½-quart baking dish. Bake for 35 to 40 minutes or until golden brown and just set in the center. Remove from oven and let stand a few minutes before serving. Serves six to eight.

COUNTRY CORN

6 slices Beef Frye
1 medium green pepper,
  chopped
1 small onion, chopped
1 17-oz. can cream-style
  corn

1 tsp. salt
1/8 tsp. cayenne pepper
4 eggs, beaten

Place Beef Frye in a 13½-inch × 8½-inch × 1¾-inch microwave-safe baking dish. Cover with paper towels. Cook Beef Frye on 50 percent power for 5 minutes or until crisp. Place 3 tablespoons Beef Frye drippings in 1½-quart microwave-safe dish. Add green peppers and onions. Continue cooking on 50 percent power for 5 minutes, stirring occasionally. Add corn, salt, cayenne pepper, and beaten eggs. Cook on 50 percent power for 8 minutes or until corn begins to thicken in center, stirring every ½ minute.

Crumble Beef Frye and sprinkle on top of casserole before serving. Serves four to six.

CRAB-CORN

6 ears fresh corn on the cob
1 3-oz. bag crab boil

salt to taste
butter or pareve margarine

In a large kettle, bring 3 quarts water to a boil. Drop ears of corn into boiling water one at a time so that water continues to boil. Add crab boil. Cover and boil until corn is tender, about 8 to 10 minutes. Remove and drain corn. Serve with butter or pareve margarine and salt to taste. Serves six.

EGGPLANT EN CASSEROLE

3 eggplants
¼ cup vegetable oil
⅔ cup minced onion
⅓ cup minced green pepper
3 garlic cloves, minced
½ lb. ground meat

3 tbsp. pareve margarine
½ tsp. sugar
¼ tsp. cayenne pepper
salt and pepper to taste
¾ cup bread crumbs
6 slivers pareve margarine

Peel, cube, and boil eggplants until tender; then drain. Heat oil in a large skillet. Add onions, green pepper, and garlic and sauté until onions are transparent, stirring frequently (about 3 minutes). Add ground meat. Cook until meat has lost its pink color. Stir often to avoid sticking. Add eggplants, pareve margarine, sugar, and seasoning. Cook for 35 minutes, stirring often.

Spoon a layer of eggplant mixture into a 1½-quart baking dish. Top with bread crumbs. Repeat layers until all eggplant mixture is used. On top layer of bread crumbs, dot with slivers of pareve margarine. Bake for 25 minutes at 350° F. or until bread crumbs are slightly browned. Serves six.

EPPES ESSEN EGGPLANT

2 medium-size onions,
  coarsely chopped
2 green peppers, chopped
2 ribs celery, thinly sliced
2 cloves garlic, minced
¼ cup olive oil
1½ tsp. basil
1¼ tsp. salt

¼ tsp. pepper
1 lb. zucchini, cut into
  chunks
1 lb. eggplant, peeled and
  cut into chunks
1 lb. tomatoes, cut into
  chunks
½ cup chopped parsley

MICROWAVE: Combine onions, green peppers, celery, garlic, and olive oil in a 4-quart glass bowl. Cover tightly with plastic wrap, turning back one edge to vent. Microwave on 100 percent power for 6 minutes, stirring once. Sprinkle with seasonings. Stir in zucchini, eggplant, and tomatoes. Cover, leaving vent, and microwave on 100 percent power for 8 minutes, then on 70 percent power for 12 minutes, stirring once during each cooking stage. Fold in parsley before serving. Serves six to eight.

CONVENTIONAL: Sauté onions, green peppers, celery, and garlic in olive oil until onion is transparent, about 10 minutes. Add zucchini and eggplant and sauté 5 minutes longer. Stir in tomatoes and seasonings. Reduce heat, cover, and simmer for 25 minutes, stirring occasionally. Fold in parsley before serving. Serves six to eight.

GATOR GREEN BEANS

4 slices Beef Frye, diced
1 onion, diced
1 clove garlic, minced
1 lb. fresh green beans,
   trimmed and cut into 1-
   inch pieces
1 tsp. salt

¼ tsp. pepper
water
2 tbsp. pareve margarine
¼ cup chopped pecans
¼ cup seasoned kosher
   bread crumbs

MICROWAVE: Combine Beef Frye and onion in a 2-quart casserole dish. Cover tightly with plastic wrap, turning back edge to vent. Microwave on 100 percent power for 5 minutes or until Beef Frye is lightly browned. Add garlic, beans, salt, pepper and ⅔ cup water. Cover, leaving vent, and microwave on 100 percent power for 13 minutes, stirring once.

In a 1-cup glass measure, combine margarine, pecans, and bread crumbs. Sprinkle on top of beans. Microwave on 70 percent power for 2 to 3 minutes or until hot and bubbly. Serves four to six.

CONVENTIONAL: Sauté Beef Frye and onion in a large saucepan until onion is transparent and Beef Frye is lightly browned. Add garlic, beans, salt, pepper, and 1 cup water. Heat to boiling. Reduce heat, cover, and simmer for 20 minutes. Transfer to a 2-quart casserole dish. Sprinkle top with mixture of pareve margarine, chopped pecans, and bread crumbs. Bake in a 375-degree oven for 8 to 10 minutes or until top is hot and bubbling. Serves four to six.

LAKE CHARLES OKRA FRITTERS

oil for deep frying
2 cups corn kernels (cut
    from about 3 ears fresh
    corn or 1 10-oz. pkg.
    frozen corn kernels,
    thawed)
2 eggs, separated
½ cup sifted cake flour

½ tsp. salt
1½ tsp. baking powder
1 tsp. sugar
½ lb. fresh okra, cut into
    ¼-inch slices (about 1
    cup)
cane syrup or honey
    (optional)

In a large heavy skillet, heat about 3 inches of oil to 400° F. for deep frying. In food processor fitted with metal blade, process 1½ cups corn kernels until puréed and smooth. Scrape the purée into a medium bowl and add the remaining corn kernels. Blend in egg yolks.

In a small bowl, combine cake flour with salt, baking powder, and sugar. Sift dry ingredients into corn mixture and stir until blended.

Beat egg whites until soft peaks form. Fold beaten egg whites into corn mixture. Stir in the okra.

Drop by heaping tablespoons into hot oil and fry, turning once, until well browned, 30 to 40 seconds. Drain on absorbent paper towels. Serve hot, drizzled with cane syrup or honey if desired. Serves four to six.

OKRA CORN-NELIA

1 tbsp. pareve margarine
1½ stalks celery, finely
    chopped
1 small onion, finely
    chopped
¼ tsp. Tabasco sauce
1 lb. kosher frankfurters,
    cut into ½-inch slices

2 cups fresh okra, trimmed
    and cut into ½-inch
    slices
½ cup chopped tomatoes
1 cup cooked kernel corn
    or 1 8-oz. can whole
    kernel corn

In a large skillet, melt pareve margarine. In food processor fitted with metal blade, process celery and onion until finely chopped. Sauté onion and celery in melted margarine until light brown. Add Tabasco sauce, sliced frankfurters, okra, tomatoes, and corn. Simmer over low flame for about 20 minutes, stirring occasionally, until okra is tender. Serves four to six.

OKRA "JAMBEAUX"

2 lbs. fresh okra, trimmed
3 tbsp. butter or pareve
  margarine
½ cup finely chopped
  onion
2 cloves garlic, finely
  chopped
½ cup finely chopped green
  pepper

3 cups coarsely chopped
  tomatoes (about 5
  medium tomatoes)
1 tsp. minced fresh parsley
1½ tsp. salt
¼ tsp. black pepper
⅛ tsp. cayenne pepper

In a food processor fitted with metal blade, process onion, garlic, and green pepper until finely chopped. In a heavy skillet, melt butter or pareve margarine. Sauté onion, garlic, and green pepper in melted butter or pareve margarine until vegetables are limp, about 6 to 8 minutes.

In processor with metal blade in place, process the tomatoes with quick on and off pulses until coarsely chopped. Do not overprocess. Add tomatoes, parsley, salt, pepper, cayenne pepper, and okra to sautéed vegetables. Cook an additional 20 minutes or until okra is tender. Serves six to eight.

ORA MAE'S BAKED ONIONS

3 large Bermuda onions,
  thickly sliced
¼ tsp. salt
¼ tsp. black pepper
⅛ tsp. cayenne pepper

¾ cup grated cheddar
  cheese
¼ cup kosher seasoned
  bread crumbs
3 tbsp. butter or margarine

Grease 1½-quart baking dish. Place onion slices in dish in a single layer. Season with salt, black pepper, and cayenne pepper. Sprinkle grated cheese over onion slices. Top with bread crumbs and dot with butter or margarine. Bake uncovered at 375° F. for about 30 minutes. Serves four.

PARADISE POTATOES

3 tbsp. butter
2 tbsp. all-purpose flour
1½ tsp. salt
½ tsp. pepper
½ tsp. paprika
1¾ or 2 cups milk
  (depending on cooking
  method)

4 medium-size potatoes,
  peeled and thinly sliced
  (about 4 cups)
1 large onion, thinly sliced

MICROWAVE: Grease a 2-quart microwave-safe ring mold. Place butter in a 4-cup glass measure. Microwave on 100 percent power for 1 minute. Stir in flour, salt, pepper, and paprika until smooth. Blend in 1¾ cups milk. Cover tightly with plastic wrap, turning back edge to vent. Microwave on 100 percent power for 5 minutes, until thickened, stirring twice. Layer potatoes and onion slices alternately in prepared mold, starting and ending with potatoes. Pour sauce over potatoes and sprinkle with additional paprika. Cover dish tightly with plastic wrap, turning back edge to vent. Microwave on 50 percent power for about 25 minutes or until potatoes are fork-tender, rotating dish twice. Let stand for 5 minutes before serving. Serves six.

CONVENTIONAL: Grease a 2-quart casserole. Preheat oven to 375° F. Melt butter in saucepan. Stir in flour, salt, pepper, and paprika until smooth. Gradually stir in 2 cups milk. Cook, stirring constantly, until thickened, about 5 minutes. Layer potatoes and onion slices alternately in prepared casserole, starting and ending with potatoes. Pour sauce over potatoes and sprinkle with additional paprika. Cover and bake for 45 minutes. Uncover and bake for 15 minutes longer or until potatoes are fork-tender. Serves six.

PAW-PAW'S STUFFED POTATOES

8 large baking potatoes
¼ cup pareve margarine
1½ cups chopped celery
1½ cups chopped green pepper
½ cup chopped shallots
2 cloves garlic, minced
1½ tsp. dried basil, crumbled
1 tsp. dried leaf thyme, crumbled

1½ lbs. cooked, cubed turkey or chicken (about 2 cups)
1½ tsp. salt
¼ tsp. cayenne pepper
2 eggs
¼ cup warm water
¼ cup warm nondairy creamer

Scrub potatoes, dry, and prick with a fork. Bake at 425° F. for 55 to 60 minutes or until done.

In a large saucepan melt pareve margarine. Add celery, green pepper, shallots, garlic, basil, and thyme. Cook for 10 to 12 minutes or until vegetables are tender. Stir in turkey or chicken, salt, and cayenne pepper.

Reduce oven temperature to 350° F. Cut a slice from top of each potato. Carefully scoop out potato without breaking the skin. Set skins aside.

In a medium mixing bowl, mash potato pulp. Beat in eggs. Combine water and nondairy creamer. Add to potato and eggs, beating until mixture is smooth. Stir in cooked vegetables. Spoon mixture into reserved potato skins. Place on a baking sheet and bake at 350° F. for 25 to 30 minutes or until heated through. Serves eight.

RED BEANS CAJUN-STYLE I

1 lb. dried red beans
½ lb. corned beef, cut into
  ¼-inch strips
1 large onion, chopped
2 tbsp. shallots, with tops,
  chopped
¼ bell pepper, chopped

3 cloves garlic, chopped
½ tsp. black pepper
½ tsp. cayenne pepper
½ tsp. Accent
1 bay leaf
about 1½ qts. water

Soak red beans in water overnight. Drain beans.

In food processor fitted with metal blade, process onion, shallots, bell pepper, and garlic with on and off pulses until vegetables are coarsely chopped.

In a 5-quart casserole dish, combine soaked beans, corned beef, onions, shallots, bell pepper, and garlic. Add seasonings and 1 quart water. Cover with lid or plastic wrap.

Microwave on High (100 percent power) for 45 minutes, stir, and add remaining water. Microwave on 50 percent power for 90 to 95 minutes or until beans are tender. A little more water may be needed from time to time to make a thick rich gravy. Let stand, covered, for 10 minutes before serving. Serves six to eight.

RED BEANS CAJUN-STYLE II

1 lb. red beans, sorted and
  washed
¾ lb. kosher smoked
  sausages, cut in ½-inch
  slices

1 medium onion, chopped
1 shallot, with tops,
  chopped
⅓ bell pepper, chopped
salt and pepper to taste

Sort and wash beans. Soak beans overnight in water to cover. In same soaking water, bring beans to a boil; lower heat and simmer for 1½ to 2 hours, stirring occasionally.

In food processor fitted with metal blade, process onion, shallot, and bell pepper until coarsely chopped. Add sausages, onion, shallot, bell pepper, salt, and pepper to beans. Simmer another 1½ hours or until beans are tender, stirring occasionally to prevent sticking. Serves six to eight.

SU-SUE'S SPINACH

1 10-oz. pkg. frozen
  spinach
8 strips Beef Frye
1 medium onion, chopped

2 tbsp. lemon juice
2 hard-cooked eggs
salt and pepper

Cook spinach according to package directions. Fry Beef Frye strips until crisp. Remove Beef Frye from pan. Add chopped onions to drippings and sauté until onions are limp and transparent.

Add lemon juice to spinach; then add spinach to onions in the pan. Cook over medium heat until most of moisture is absorbed, about 10 to 15 minutes, stirring frequently.

Break Beef Frye into bits and add to spinach just before serving. Transfer to serving dish and garnish with slices of hard-cooked eggs. Add salt and pepper to taste. Serves four.

VEGETABLES C'EST BON

2 cups broccoli flowerets
1 cup cauliflower flowerets
2 tbsp. water
1 medium zucchini, sliced
  ¼ inch thick
1 cup fresh mushrooms

1 green pepper, cut into
  thin strips
¼ lb. butter or pareve
  margarine, melted
juice from 1 lemon

On a large microwave-safe platter, arrange broccoli and cauliflower around outer edge. Sprinkle with water. Cover with plastic wrap, leaving a small area unsealed at the edge. Microwave on High (100 percent power) for 2 minutes. Place zucchini, mushrooms, and peppers in center. Cook, covered, on High for 3 to 5 minutes or until vegetables are crisp-tender. Drain off liquid. Combine melted butter or pareve margarine and lemon juice. Drizzle over vegetables just before serving. Serves six.

Mamou
FOWL

When a Cajun fiddler in Mamou starts to strum, along with the "chang-a-lang" (triangle) and the accordion, your feet start tapping. Before long you are gliding and dancing across the floor to the rhythm of Cajun music. Even the strange name of the small rural town, Mamou, has a lilt to it, an almost rhythmic quality. This town in southwestern Louisiana is a prime source of authentic Cajun music. The town lures the traveler not by its sights but rather by its sounds. The sounds say, "Here is traditional Cajun music at its best."

Cajun music evolved from several influences. The music of the early settlers was basically French folk music sung occasionally to the accompaniment of a simple string instrument like the fiddle. Later American folk music, the blues and jazz of nearby New Orleans, and even the Germans (who introduced the accordion to Cajun music) all helped create the sounds of this kind of music as we know it today.

Cajuns learn to dance at a very early age and it is not unusual to see young children joining in on the dance floor. In fact, it was children that gave rise to the expression "fais do do" or "go to sleep." When the early Cajuns gathered together for their dances, an area around the dance floor was set aside for the children to be put to sleep, where they remained under the watchful eye of their parents.

Cajun music, like Cajun food, was a blend of whatever was available. While the flavor of Cajun food was dictated by the abundance and proximity of herbs, spices, wildlife, and seafood, Cajun music was equally affected by the sounds and rhythms that drifted up from nearby cities. Not far to the southeast was New Orleans with its heralded blues and jazz musicians and from the Prairie Cajuns west of the Atchafalaya Basin nearer to Lafayette, came the strains of bluegrass and country music.

The combination of good food and good music put the town of Mamou on the map. Today, Mamou can hardly be considered a dusty rural town, for as soon as the dust settles, the Cajuns are there, beckoning all to join in the feasting and feting. And as the music begins, the dancers kick up their heels and "la poussière" (the dust) begins to fly.

FOWL

Abie-Gator Casserole *(Conventional and Processor)*
Beaux-B-Q Chicken *(Microwave)*
Chang-a-Lang Chicken *(Conventional and Processor)*
Chicken Nu-Getz *(Conventional)*
Co-hens Stew *(Microwave and Processor)*
Cora Belle's Cornish Hens *(Conventional)*
Desirée's Baked Duck *(Microwave)*
Duckling à l'Orange *(Microwave and Conventional)*
Fais Do Do Fritters *(Conventional)*
Fiddlers' Jambalaya *(Microwave, Processor, and Conventional)*
Folksy Fowl *(Conventional)*
Gabbai's Gobbler *(Microwave and Conventional)*
Katy's Krunchy Chicken *(Microwave)*
Luz-i-ana Lemon Chicken *(Conventional)*
Mamou's Coq Au Vin *(Conventional)*
Nuch-a Southern Fried Chicken *(Conventional)*
Paysan's Poulet *(Conventional)*
Poulet mit Pasta *(Conventional)*
Ragin' Cajun Cabobs *(Conventional)*
Traditional Turkey with Dressing *(Conventional)*

ABIE-GATOR CASSEROLE

5 tbsp. pareve margarine
1 small onion, chopped
3 cloves garlic, chopped
3 shallots, chopped
3 ribs celery, chopped
2 cups ground turkey
1 beaten egg
1 tsp. salt

¼ tsp. black pepper
¼ tsp. cayenne pepper
3 mirlitons, peeled, cubed,
  cooked, and drained
3 slices bread, moistened,
  drained, and squeezed
1 tbsp. chopped parsley
seasoned bread crumbs

Melt 2 tablespoons pareve margarine in skillet. In food processor fitted with metal blade place onion, garlic, shallots, and celery. With quick on and off pulses, process vegetables until finely chopped. Sauté vegetables in pareve margarine together with ground turkey for 6 minutes. Set aside in a 2-quart baking dish. To skillet add egg, salt, peppers, mirlitons, remaining pareve margarine, and bread. Mix and cook for 10 minutes on medium-low heat. Stir in parsley. Add to mixture in baking dish and mix well. Sprinkle with bread crumbs. Bake at 350° F. until crumbs are slightly browned. Serves ten to twelve.

BEAUX-B-Q CHICKEN

1 3-lb. fryer, cut into
  quarters
salt and pepper
¼ cup hot water
2 small onions, sliced
¾ cup tomato juice
⅛ tsp. cayenne pepper
1 tsp. salt

⅛ tsp. black pepper
½ tsp. prepared mustard
2 tsp. Worcestershire sauce
1 bay leaf
1 tbsp. sugar
1 clove garlic
6 tbsp. vinegar
1 tbsp. pareve margarine

Arrange chicken quarters, skin side down, in a 10-inch microwave-safe skillet. Salt and pepper generously. Pour hot water into skillet;

then arrange onions over chicken. Cook, uncovered, on 50 percent power for 8 minutes.

While chicken is cooking, combine remaining ingredients in a 2-cup glass measuring cup. Then set chicken aside and heat sauce in microwave on 50 percent power for 3 minutes. Pour sauce over chicken. Return chicken to microwave and cook, uncovered, on 50 percent power for about 25 minutes. Turn chicken and baste with sauce several times during cooking period.

Preheat conventional oven to 425° F. Transfer cooked chicken to conventional oven for 8 to 10 minutes or until chicken is nicely glazed and fork-tender. Serves four.

CHANG-A-LANG CHICKEN

2 medium (2½-lb.)
  chickens, cut into 8
  pieces each
1½ cups pecans
1 cup all-purpose flour
1 cup cornmeal
4 tsp. paprika
2 tsp. salt

2 tsp. black pepper
2 tsp. cayenne pepper
4 eggs
½ cup water
4 cups corn oil
Honey Pecan Sauce (see
  recipe), optional

Wash chicken pieces well and pat dry. In food processor fitted with steel blade, finely chop pecans. Add flour, cornmeal, paprika, salt, pepper, and cayenne pepper to processor and pulse once or twice until pecans are well blended with seasonings. Do not overprocess.

In a separate bowl, mix eggs and water. Dip chicken pieces into egg mixture, then into dry mixture, covering each piece evenly.

Heat corn oil in a large, deep frying pan. Add chicken pieces and fry about 10 minutes on each side. Add more oil if necessary. Drain on paper towels. Dip chicken in hot Honey Pecan Sauce if desired. Serves six.

CHICKEN NU-GETZ

6 chicken breasts
2 eggs
1 cup water
1 cup flour
3 tbsp. sesame seeds
1 tsp. salt

¼ tsp. cayenne pepper
1 tsp. Accent
vegetable oil for frying
Nippy Fruit Sauce or Sauce
 Royale (see recipes)

Cut chicken from bone and cut into 1-inch × 1½-inch nuggets. Mix eggs and water; add flour, sesame seeds, salt, pepper, and Accent to make a batter.

Fill heavy skillet one-third full with oil. Heat over medium heat until temperature reaches 375° F. for deep frying. Dip nuggets into batter; drain off excess batter. Add nuggets to hot oil. Fry for 3 to 5 minutes or until golden brown and well done. Drain on paper towels. Serve with Nippy Fruit Sauce and/or Sauce Royale. Serves six.

CO-HENS STEW

1 3-lb. fryer, cut into pieces
½ tsp. garlic powder
½ tsp. white pepper
½ tsp. black pepper
½ tsp. red pepper
¼ tsp. dry mustard
¼ tsp. crushed basil
½ cup nondairy creamer
2¼ cups water
½ cup flour

1 tbsp. vegetable oil
1 large onion, chopped
3 shallots, chopped
3 ribs celery, chopped
1 small bell pepper,
 chopped
3 cloves garlic, chopped
1 tbsp. pareve margarine
1 tbsp. Worcestershire
 sauce

In food processor fitted with metal blade, place onion, shallots, celery, bell pepper, and garlic. Process with on and off pulses until vegetables are coarsely chopped. Set aside.

Preheat the microwave browning skillet on High for 7 minutes. Meanwhile, blend together garlic powder, white pepper, black pepper, red pepper, dry mustard, and basil. Sprinkle over chicken. Combine nondairy creamer with ¼ cup water. Dip chicken in liquid and then flour and set aside.

Place oil in preheated microwave browning skillet and place chicken pieces in skillet. Microwave on High for 5 minutes; turn and microwave on High for 5 to 7 minutes or until browned. Set aside.

In a 4-cup glass measure, combine chopped vegetables and pareve margarine. Microwave on High for 3 to 4 minutes or until vegetables are soft but not brown. In a 5-quart casserole, combine vegetables, chicken, Worcestershire sauce, and 2 cups water. Cover with plastic wrap. Microwave on High for 15 minutes, stir, and microwave on 50 percent power for 30 to 35 minutes or until chicken is done. Let stand, covered, for 10 minutes before serving. Serves four to six.

CORA BELLE'S CORNISH HENS

6 Cornish hens
salt and pepper to taste
1 cup wild rice or brown
  rice
2 onions, chopped
1 cup boiling water
¼ lb. fresh mushrooms, cut
  up or 1 4-oz. can
  mushroom stems and
  pieces

¼ lb. pareve margarine
¼ tsp. poultry seasoning
1 tsp. paprika

Rinse and pat dry hens. Rub salt and pepper inside and out. Rinse rice in cold water and drain well. Brown onions in margarine. Add raw rice and continue to brown. Add boiling water and cook, on low heat, for 20 minutes or until liquid is absorbed. Add mushrooms and poultry seasoning.

Stuff hens with rice mixture. Sprinkle paprika over hens. Bake in open roasting pan at 325° F. for 1 to 1½ hours or until hens are fork-tender and brown. Baste often. Serves six.

DESIRÉE'S BAKED DUCK

1 5- to 7-lb. duck, cut in
  half
Kitchen Bouquet browning
  sauce
½ tsp. salt
½ tsp. white pepper
¼ tsp. black pepper
½ tsp. cayenne pepper

¼ tsp. garlic powder
½ tsp. onion powder
½ tsp. paprika
½ tsp. dried thyme
¾ cup melted pareve
  margarine
¾ cup water

Wash duck and pat dry. Rub with Kitchen Bouquet browning sauce. Combine all seasonings. Sprinkle over duck. Place duck halves, skin side down, on microwave roasting rack in 8-inch × 12-inch glass baking dish. Baste with mixture of melted margarine and water. Cover with wax paper.

Microwave on 70 percent power for 20 minutes, baste, and turn skin side up. Cover with wax paper. Microwave on 70 percent power for 25 to 30 minutes or until juices run clear and duck is fork-tender. Baste and let stand, covered, for 5 minutes before serving. Serves four.

DUCKLING À L'ORANGE

1 5-lb. duckling
salt and pepper
½ cup fresh orange juice
grated peel of 1 orange
½ cup dry white wine
⅓ cup sugar
2 tbsp. Sabra liqueur

1 tbsp. lemon juice
1 tbsp. cornstarch
½ tsp. Kitchen Bouquet
  browning sauce (optional)
orange slices or wedges for
  garnish
parsley sprigs for garnish

MICROWAVE: Rinse duckling well. Sprinkle with salt and pepper. Prick skin in several places to allow fat to drain during cooking. Place duckling, breast side down, on microwave-safe rack in microwave-safe roasting pan. Cover tightly with plastic wrap, turning back edge to vent. Microwave on 70 percent power for 20 minutes, rotating dish once. Turn duckling breast side up. Microwave, uncovered, on 70 percent power for 14 to 16 minutes longer or until microwave-safe meat thermometer reads 185° F. when inserted into thickest part of breast or joint between thigh and body.

Preheat broiler. Cut duckling into quarters. Broil, skin side up, for 8 to 10 minutes or until well browned.

Meanwhile, combine orange juice, orange peel, wine, sugar, liqueur, lemon juice, cornstarch, and browning sauce if used in a 2-cup glass measure. Cover tightly with plastic wrap, turning back edge to vent. Microwave on 100 percent power for 4 minutes, stirring twice.

Place duckling on a platter and spoon a little sauce over. Place remaining sauce in a gravy boat. Garnish with orange slices or wedges and parsley sprigs. Serves four.

CONVENTIONAL: Preheat oven to 350° F. Rinse duckling well. Sprinkle with salt and pepper. Prick skin in several places to allow fat to drain during cooking. Place duckling on rack in roasting pan. Roast, covered, for 2 hours. Remove cover and roast for 30 minutes more or until meat is tender and well browned.

Meanwhile, combine orange juice, orange peel, wine, sugar, liqueur, lemon juice, cornstarch, and browning sauce if used in a small saucepan. Heat to boiling, stirring constantly. Boil for 1 minute.

Cut duckling into quarters, place on a platter and spoon a little sauce over. Place remaining sauce in a gravy boat. Garnish with orange slices or wedges and parsley sprigs. Serves four.

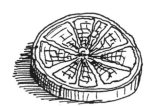

FAIS DO DO FRITTERS

2 eggs, separated
2 cups cooked chopped
  turkey
½ cup minced celery

1 tsp. grated onion
¼ cup flour
½ tsp. salt
2 tbsp. vegetable oil

Mix egg yolks with turkey, celery, onion, flour, and salt. Beat egg whites until stiff. Fold into turkey mixture. Drop mixture from a large spoon into heated vegetable oil. Brown on both sides. Drain on absorbent paper. Makes six to eight.

FIDDLERS' JAMBALAYA

1 large onion, chopped
2 shallots, chopped
1 green pepper, chopped
1 stalk celery, chopped
2 cloves garlic, minced
½ cup diced Polish sausage
¼ cup olive oil
1 28-oz. can stewed
  tomatoes

1⅓ cups chicken broth
1 cup instant rice
1 tsp. minced parsley
½ tsp. thyme
½ tsp. salt
½ tsp. black pepper
¼ tsp. Tabasco sauce
1 3-lb. fryer, cut up
1 tbsp. paprika

MICROWAVE: In food processor fitted with metal blade, process onion, shallots, green pepper, celery, and garlic with on and off pulses until vegetables are chopped. Combine chopped vegetables, diced sausage, and olive oil in a 4-quart casserole. Cover tightly with plastic wrap, turning back edge to vent. Microwave on 100 percent power for 8 minutes, stirring once. Stir in tomatoes, chicken broth, rice, parsley, thyme, salt, pepper, and Tabasco sauce.

Sprinkle chicken with paprika. Add to casserole, placing thicker pieces at edge of dish. Cover, leaving vent, and microwave on 100 percent power for 35 minutes, stirring once. Cover and microwave on

70 percent power for 3 minutes. Let stand for 5 minutes before serving. Serves six.

CONVENTIONAL: In food processor fitted with metal blade, process onion, shallots, green pepper, celery, and garlic with on and off pulses until vegetables are chopped. Set aside.

Rub chicken with paprika. Brown chicken in olive oil in large skillet. Remove chicken from pan. Add chopped vegetables. Sauté until onion is transparent, about 10 minutes. Stir in diced sausage, tomatoes, chicken broth, rice, and seasonings. Add chicken and spoon sauce over it. Heat to boiling. Reduce heat, cover, and simmer for 30 minutes or until chicken is tender. Serves six.

FOLKSY FOWL

1 5- to 6-lb. roasting chicken	**½ tsp. pepper**
2 large onions	**¼ tsp. garlic powder**
2 tbsp. pareve margarine, melted	**½ cup ketchup**
½ tsp. salt	**⅛ tsp. Tabasco sauce**
	¾ cup water

Cut up onions and place in bottom of roasting pan. Place chicken on top of onions. Brush chicken with melted margarine. Sprinkle with salt, pepper, and garlic powder. Place, covered, in a 350-degree oven for 30 minutes.

Mix together ketchup, Tabasco, and water until well blended. Pour over chicken and roast for 1½ hours more or until chicken is tender. Remove cover and continue roasting, basting occasionally, for an additional 30 minutes or until chicken is well browned. Serves six to eight.

GABBAI'S GOBBLER

1 5-lb. frozen turkey breast, thawed
¼ cup pareve margarine
1 medium-size onion, chopped
½ lb. fresh mushrooms, sliced
2 cups long-grain rice
1 10-oz. can condensed chicken soup, undiluted

½ tsp. thyme
1 tsp. salt
¼ tsp. pepper
½ cup dry white wine
¾ cup water, for conventional method only

MICROWAVE: Place turkey breast skin side down in a deep 4-quart casserole. Cover tightly with plastic wrap, turning back edge to vent. Microwave on 100 percent power for 20 minutes.

In a glass bowl, combine pareve margarine, onion, and mushrooms. Cover tightly with plastic wrap, turning back edge to vent. Microwave on 100 percent power for 5 minutes, stirring twice. Add rice, cover, leaving vent, and microwave on 100 percent power for 3 minutes. Stir in chicken soup, thyme, salt, pepper, and wine.

Turn turkey skin side up. Pour rice mixture around turkey. Cover, leaving vent, and microwave on 70 percent power for 30 to 35 minutes or until internal temperature reaches 175° F. Stir rice and rotate casserole once during cooking. Let stand, covered, for 5 minutes before serving. Serves eight.

CONVENTIONAL: Preheat oven to 325° F. In a skillet, sauté onion and mushrooms in pareve margarine until onion is transparent. Add rice and cook, stirring, until rice is lightly browned. Stir in chicken soup, thyme, salt, pepper, wine, and water.

Place turkey breast, skin side up, in a deep 4-quart casserole. Pour rice mixture around turkey breast. Cover tightly and bake 2 hours or until internal temperature reaches 180° F. Let stand for 15 minutes before serving. Serves eight.

KATY'S KRUNCHY CHICKEN

⅓ cup pareve margarine
1 clove garlic, finely
    chopped
¾ cup bread crumbs
1 tbsp. dried parsley flakes

1 tsp. salt
¼ tsp. poultry seasoning
⅛ tsp. cayenne pepper
1 2½- to 3-lb. fryer, cut up

Place pareve margarine and garlic in a 2-quart glass baking dish. Microwave on 70 percent power for about 2 minutes or until margarine is melted. Combine remaining ingredients except chicken in a flat dish. Roll chicken in seasoned margarine, then in crumb mixture. Place chicken pieces, skin side up and meaty pieces toward outside, in baking dish. Sprinkle with remaining bread crumbs. Cover with wax paper.

Microwave on 100 percent power for 12 minutes. Turn chicken over and continue cooking on 100 percent power for 10 to 12 minutes or until tender. Let stand for 5 minutes before serving. Serves six.

LUZ-I-ANA LEMON CHICKEN

3 chicken breasts, boned
  and halved
3 tbsp. pareve margarine
1 tbsp. flour
¼ tsp. salt
¼ tsp. cayenne pepper
1 tsp. tarragon
1 tsp. oregano
¼ tsp. garlic powder

¼ tsp. onion powder
⅛ tsp. thyme
1 chicken bouillon cube
½ cup hot water
1 tbsp. hot prepared
  mustard
6 lemon slices
1 tbsp. parsley flakes

Melt pareve margarine in a large skillet over high heat. Combine flour with seasonings and mix well. Coat chicken on all sides with seasoned flour. Place chicken in skillet and cook for 5 minutes, stirring constantly. Dissolve bouillon cube in water; add to chicken with mustard and lemon slices. Stir to loosen particles from the bottom of the pan. Cover and cook for 3 to 5 minutes or until chicken breasts are tender. Sprinkle with parsley flakes just before serving. Serves four to six.

MAMOU'S COQ AU VIN

1 roasting chicken (about 6
  lbs.), cut in pieces
1 tsp. salt
¼ tsp. cayenne pepper
2 tbsp. flour
3 tbsp. vegetable oil
6 whole small onions
1 clove garlic, minced

1 4-oz. can sliced
  mushrooms
1½ to 2 cups red wine
1 large bay leaf
¼ cup minced parsley
3 shallots, with tops, sliced
  into thin pieces

Mix flour with salt and cayenne pepper. Coat chicken on all sides with seasoned flour. Brown in a heavy skillet in hot vegetable oil.

Remove chicken with slotted spoon and set aside. Add onions and garlic to skillet and cook until onions are transparent and tender. Add remaining ingredients and chicken pieces. Cover; simmer for 2 hours or until chicken is fork-tender. Serves six.

NUCH-A SOUTHERN FRIED CHICKEN

1 2½- to 3-lb. fryer, cut into
  pieces
½ cup flour
½ tsp. salt
¼ tsp. black pepper

¼ tsp. cayenne pepper
1 tsp. paprika
¼ tsp. garlic powder
vegetable oil for frying

Mix flour with seasonings. Coat chicken with flour mixture on all sides. Heat oil in a heavy skillet until moderately hot (350° F.). Add chicken, cover, and cook for 10 to 15 minutes. When golden brown, turn. Reduce heat. Finish cooking uncovered, turning as needed, until brown and crisp on all sides. Drain on paper towels. Serves four.

PAYSAN'S POULET

1 2½- to 3-lb. fryer, cut up
  and skin removed
½ cup Russian, Italian, or
  French salad dressing

1 tsp. onion powder
½ tsp. cayenne pepper
½ tsp. garlic powder
1½ cups cracker crumbs

Combine salad dressing with seasonings. Brush chicken with dressing and coat with crumbs. Place on rack of broiler pan. Bake at 400° F. for 45 to 50 minutes or until chicken is tender. Serves four.

POULET MIT PASTA

8 oz. rotelle macaroni
4 tbsp. olive oil
2 whole skinless, boneless
  chicken breasts, cut into
  bite-size pieces
3 tbsp. all-purpose flour
1 16-oz. can whole
  tomatoes
1 large red bell pepper,
  seeded and cut into ½-
  inch strips

1 large green bell pepper,
  seeded and cut into ½-
  inch strips
1 medium-size onion, diced
¼ tsp. salt
¼ tsp. cayenne pepper
⅛ tsp. black pepper
¼ tsp. garlic powder

In a covered deep 4-quart saucepan over high heat, bring 2 quarts water to a boil. Add macaroni and cook for 12 to 15 minutes, stirring frequently, until tender.

Meanwhile, in a deep 12-inch skillet, over medium-high heat, heat 2 tablespoons olive oil; add chicken pieces and cook for about 5 minutes, stirring frequently until chicken is browned on all sides and cooked through. Remove chicken to bowl; keep warm.

Heat remaining olive oil in skillet; stir in flour. Cook for 5 minutes, stirring constantly until flour is dark brown, forming a good roux. Do not allow flour to burn. Stir in tomatoes with their liquid, peppers, onion, salt, cayenne pepper, black pepper, and garlic powder. Reduce heat to medium. Cook about 5 minutes, stirring occasionally, until vegetables are tender and mixture is slightly thickened. Drain rotelle; add to skillet along with chicken. Stir until well mixed. Serves four.

RAGIN' CAJUN CABOBS

4 Italian-kosher sausages
¼ cup dry white wine
¼ cup hot mustard
1 large clove garlic, crushed
2 tbsp. olive oil
2 tsp. Worcestershire sauce
½ tsp. dried thyme
¼ tsp. salt
⅛ tsp. ground pepper

2 whole boneless chicken
breasts, skinned, cut into
32 pieces
2 small zucchini, cut into
32 rounds
4 medium bell peppers,
quartered lengthwise,
then halved crosswise

In a covered skillet cook sausages in ¼-inch of water over medium heat until cooked through (about 15 minutes). Cut each sausage into 8 pieces and set aside.

Combine wine, mustard, garlic, oil, Worcestershire sauce, thyme, salt, and pepper in a medium bowl. Add pieces of sausage and chicken and stir to coat. Chill, covered, for 4 hours or overnight.

Heat broiler or grill. Thread sausage, zucchini, chicken and bell peppers (in that order) on 16 skewers. Broil 5 inches from heat, turning occasionally, until sausage is browned and chicken is cooked through (about 8 to 10 minutes). Serves sixteen.

TRADITIONAL TURKEY
WITH DRESSING

1 12- to 15-lb. turkey
½ tsp. salt
¼ tsp. black pepper
¼ tsp. cayenne pepper
1 medium-size onion
½ medium bell pepper
1 rib celery
½ loaf stale bread

2 shallots, with tops,
  chopped
1 clove garlic, minced
½ tsp. dried parsley flakes
⅛ tsp. oregano
⅛ tsp. thyme
4 tbsp. pareve margarine
juice of ½ lemon

Wash turkey thoroughly inside and out. Dry well. Season inside and out with salt, black pepper, and cayenne pepper. Take turkey liver and broil it under open flame until done. Take neck and gizzard and boil in a saucepan in water seasoned with salt and pepper. When tender, remove from fire. Reserve liquid. Remove skin from the neck and remove all neck meat. Set aside with liver and gizzard. Grind neck meat, liver, and gizzard along with onion, bell pepper, celery, shallots, and garlic.

Crumble bread into a large bowl. Moisten bread with broth from boiling neck and gizzards until mixture will hold shape enough for you to handle. Add ground meat mixture and mix well. Season mixture with parsley, oregano, and thyme. Stuff lightly into body and neck cavity of turkey. Sew up cavities.

Melt margarine in a saucepan with lemon juice. Brush over entire turkey, front and back. Place turkey on rack in roaster pan. Dust lightly with flour. Cover pan tightly with aluminum foil. Bake in a preheated 350-degree oven for 3½ to 4 hours, allowing about 30 minutes to the pound. When cooked, remove foil and continue baking, uncovered, for about 30 minutes or until turkey is nicely browned. Serves twelve to fifteen.

Opelousas
YAMS (SWEET POTATOES)

Opelousas, the Yam Capital of Louisiana, a city of gracious living, friendly and hospitable, extends a hearty welcome to all visitors. Situated in the state's St. Landry Parish, Opelousas served as a sanctuary for Acadian exiles after their expulsion from Nova Scotia in 1755. Much of the life style of the Acadians, better known today as Cajuns, has been preserved here. Their spirit and their customs (the fais do do, the boucherie, the coupe de main, and the chari-vari) are still very much a part of family life in Opelousas.

In Opelousas, many opulent and famous homes, dating back to the pre-Civil War period, are set amidst moss-hung oaks, ancient pines, and cedar trees. They are among the city's main tourist attractions. Not to be missed is the picturesque Estorge House, "the elegant old lady of Market Street." Built by slaves in the 1820s, it has been occupied by generations of the same family. Another "must see" attraction is the Opelousas Jim Bowie House, a free museum. Opelousas likes to claim an important part in shaping the character of the flamboyant Jim Bowie.

Opelousas is the land of the very special sweet potato known as the moist Golden Yam of Louisiana. The story and success of the sweet potato industry began almost by accident. It was the failure of the cotton crop around World War I that led the farmers to grow sweet potatoes for profit. By the 1930s the sweet potatoes were beginning to flourish, and this unique Louisiana product gained recognition in the nation's agriculture market. By 1946 Opelousas was grateful to the sweet potato, now developed through extensive and careful scientific research into the moist and golden Louisiana yams, and called it the "black gold of oil."

At the peak of the harvest season, around the first week of October, an annual sweet potato festival called the Yambilee is held. In recognition of the once-lowly sweet potato, the festival publicizes, glorifies, and glamorizes the yam. Gigantic and colorful parades are held. Young ladies throughout the state vie for the title of Sweet Potato Queen. The festival climaxes with the coronation of the queen surrounded by "yam land" royalty.

Since the days when gallant explorers paddled their pirogues through the bayous, Opelousas has been a land of happy Cajun laughter, of good living and of good eating. No one knew good eating better than the Cajun housewife. She took the popular, nourishing, and economical vegetable the yam and proved its versatility in the kitchen.

Ask any Opelousas native about the virtues of their famous Golden Yam and you are likely to hear the words "bon bouche" – it's something you save for the last delicious bite.

YAMS
(SWEET POTATOES)

Auntée's Sweet Potato Salad *(Conventional)*
Bon Bouche Cheesecake *(Processor and Conventional)*
Cajun Country Yam Pie *(Processor and Conventional)*
Couzon's Confection *(Conventional)*
Frumie's French Fries *(Conventional)*
Gaston's Griddle Cakes *(Conventional)*
Golda's Glazed Yams *(Microwave)*
Jim Bowie's Yam Bake *(Microwave and Conventional)*
Orange Yams Opelousas I *(Microwave)*
Orange Yams Opelousas II *(Processor and Conventional)*
Parish Potato Soufflé *(Processor and Conventional)*
Plain Ol' Yams *(Microwave)*
Sorchée's Sweet Potato Biscuits *(Conventional)*
Southland Sweet Potatoes *(Microwave)*
Sweet Potato Soup *(Conventional and Processor)*
Yambilee Fritters *(Conventional)*
Yamland Muffins *(Conventional)*
Yam Latkes *(Conventional)*
Yam Waldorf Salad *(Conventional)*
Yente's Yam and Sausage Supper *(Conventional)*

AUNTÉE'S SWEET POTATO SALAD

4 large sweet potatoes,
   cooked, peeled, and
   cubed
1 cup sour cream
¼ cup chopped parsley
1 tbsp. lemon juice
1 tsp. sugar
1 tsp. salt

½ tsp. celery seeds
¼ tsp. paprika
¼ tsp. crushed dill
¼ tsp. pepper
1 cup chopped celery
1 shallot, white part only,
   chopped
lettuce leaves

Place cubed potatoes in a large bowl. In another bowl, combine sour cream, parsley, lemon juice, sugar, salt, celery seeds, paprika, dill, and pepper, blending well. Add celery and shallots to potatoes. Divide sour cream mixture in half. Take half of mixture, cover, and refrigerate. Add other half of sour cream mixture to potato mixture, stirring until evenly coated. Chill well, for 2 hours or more. Serve over lettuce leaves. Use remaining sour cream mixture as topping. Serves six.

BON BOUCHE CHEESECAKE

1⅔ cups graham cracker
  crumbs
⅓ cup butter or margarine,
  melted
2 envelopes unflavored
  kosher gelatin
½ cup cold water
3 eggs, separated
¾ cup sugar
½ tsp. salt
⅓ cup milk

2 8-oz. pkgs. cream cheese,
  softened
1¼ cups cooked, mashed
  sweet potatoes
1 cup whipping cream,
  whipped
½ tsp. vanilla extract
additional whipped cream
  (optional)
mandarin orange slices
  (optional)

Combine graham cracker crumbs and melted butter or margarine. Mix well. Press into bottom and 1½ inches up sides of a 9-inch springform pan. Chill.

Soften gelatin in cold water in top of a double boiler. Stir in egg yolks, sugar, salt, and milk. Place over water and bring water to a boil. Reduce heat; then cook, stirring constantly, until slightly thickened. Add cream cheese and sweet potatoes. Pour mixture into food processor fitted with metal blade. Process until mixture is smooth.

Beat egg whites until they are stiff and hold peaks. Fold egg whites, whipped cream, and vanilla into sweet potato mixture. Spoon into prepared pan. Chill until set. Garnish with additional whipped cream and orange slices, if desired. Serves eight to ten.

CAJUN COUNTRY YAM PIE

1 16-oz. can mashed yams
½ cup brown sugar
¼ cup granulated sugar
¼ cup cornstarch
1 egg yolk
¼ cup margarine, softened

1 tbsp. grated orange rind
¼ tsp. salt
½ tsp. cinnamon
½ cup chopped pecans
1 9-inch unbaked pie shell

Preheat oven to 350° F. Place yams, brown sugar, white sugar, cornstarch, egg yolk, margarine, orange rind, salt, and spices in food processor fitted with metal blade. Pulse on and off until yam mixture is smooth. Pour into unbaked pie shell. Sprinkle top with chopped pecans. Bake for 50 minutes or until steel knife inserted into pie comes out clean. Serves six to eight.

COUZON'S CONFECTION

2 cups sugar
½ cup evaporated milk
1 cup pecans

½ cup cooked yams
½ stick butter or margarine
½ tsp. vanilla extract

Bring sugar and milk to a boil. Add pecans and yams. Cook until mixture starts to sugar. Remove from fire and add butter and vanilla. Cover and let cool. Beat well and pour into a buttered dish or shallow pan. When cold, break into serving pieces. Makes about one pound.

FRUMIE'S FRENCH FRIES

3 medium-size sweet
potatoes

vegetable oil for deep frying
½ to ¾ cup powdered sugar

Cook sweet potatoes in boiling water for 10 minutes. Let cool to touch. Peel and cut into finger-size strips or ¼-inch slices. Fry in hot oil (380° F.) until golden brown. Drain on paper towels. Sprinkle with powdered sugar while hot. Serves four to six.

GASTON'S GRIDDLE CAKES

1½ cups sifted flour
3½ tsp. baking powder
1 tsp. salt
½ tsp. cinnamon
2 eggs, well beaten

1½ cups milk
¼ cup melted butter
1¼ cups mashed cooked
    yams

Sift dry ingredients into a mixing bowl. Combine eggs, milk, and butter. Add gradually to dry ingredients. Stir only until batter is smooth. Stir in mashed yams.

Drop by tablespoonful onto hot buttered griddle. Cook slowly until surface is covered with bubbles; turn and cook until bottom is browned. Serve with additional butter and honey or syrup if desired. Makes about twelve.

GOLDA'S GLAZED YAMS

4 medium cooked yams,
    peeled and cut into
    1-inch slices

¼ cup butter or pareve
    margarine
½ cup brown sugar

Combine butter or pareve margarine and brown sugar in a 1½-quart microwave casserole. Microwave on Medium (50 percent power) for 30 to 60 seconds or until bubbling. Add yam slices and toss lightly to coat with sugar mixture. Cover. Cook on Medium for 5 to 7 minutes or until heated through. Serves six.

JIM BOWIE'S YAM BAKE

1 lb. sweet potatoes,
    peeled (2 medium-size
    potatoes)
3 small apples, cored and
    sliced
¾ cup orange juice
¼ cup firmly packed dark
    brown sugar

1 tbsp. lemon juice
¾ tsp. salt
½ tsp. cinnamon
1 tbsp. butter or pareve
    margarine
⅓ cup chopped pecans

MICROWAVE METHOD: Grease a 1½-quart casserole dish. Slice sweet potatoes and layer alternately with apples in prepared casserole. Mix orange juice, brown sugar, lemon juice, salt, and cinnamon. Pour over potatoes and apples. Dot with butter or pareve margarine and sprinkle with chopped pecans. Cover tightly with plastic wrap, turning back one edge to vent. Microwave on 100 percent power for 18 minutes or until potatoes are fork-tender, spooning sauce over and rotating casserole twice. Let stand, covered, for 5 minutes before serving. Serves six.

CONVENTIONAL METHOD: Grease a 1½-quart casserole dish. Preheat oven to 350° F. Slice sweet potatoes and assemble casserole as directed in microwave method. Bake for 40 to 45 minutes or until potatoes are fork-tender, basting with sauce once or twice during cooking. Serves six.

ORANGE YAMS OPELOUSAS I

3 large oranges
4 medium sweet potatoes
1 tbsp. butter or pareve
    margarine

¼ cup brown sugar
½ tsp. salt
¾ cup orange juice
6 kosher marshmallows

Cut oranges in half. Juice oranges and measure ¾ cup juice; set aside. Remove membrane from orange halves, wash shells, and reserve.

Scrub potatoes and prick all the way through with a large fork. Place on a paper towel laid in bottom of microwave oven. Bake on Medium (50 percent power) for 15 to 18 minutes or until potatoes are well done. Turn potatoes about halfway through cooking time.

Peel hot sweet potatoes, mash, and season with butter or pareve margarine, brown sugar, and salt. Whip until light and fluffy, while gradually adding orange juice. Fill six orange shells with sweet potato mixture and place in a 6½-inch × 10-inch × 1¾-inch (1½-quart) glass dish. Top each serving with a whole kosher marshmallow. Bake in microwave on 50 percent power for an additional 5 minutes. Place under broiler element for a few seconds to brown marshmallows. Serves six to eight.

ORANGE YAMS OPELOUSAS II

3 large oranges
2 16-oz. cans yams, drained
¼ cup orange juice
⅓ cup packed light brown
    sugar

¼ cup butter or pareve
    margarine, melted
6 kosher marshmallows
6 Maraschino cherries for
    garnish (optional)

Cut oranges into halves; squeeze, reserving ¼ cup juice. Carefully remove pulp from orange shells; make scalloped design on edges of orange shells, if desired, using sharp paring knife.

Place yams in food processor fitted with steel blade. Pulse for about 30 seconds or until yams are smooth. Add orange juice, brown sugar, and 3 tablespoons melted butter or pareve margarine. Pulse once or twice to combine all ingredients.

Using a pastry tube fitted with large star tip, pipe yam mixture into orange shells. Brush edges of shells with remaining butter or pareve margarine. Place filled shells in a shallow baking pan. Bake at 350° F. until hot through, about 20 minutes. Place marshmallow on each orange shell. Bake an additional 10 minutes or until marshmallow has melted. Garnish with cherry on each orange shell before serving, if desired. Serves six.

PARISH POTATO SOUFFLÉ

2 lbs. yams, peeled and cut into quarters (about 4 medium-size potatoes)
½ tsp. cinnamon
¾ tsp. salt
dash cloves
2 tbsp. sugar
2 tbsp. butter or pareve margarine
1 egg

¼ cup heavy cream or nondairy creamer
1 2-inch square orange peel
1 2-inch square lemon peel
¼ cup brown sugar (optional)
1 tbsp. additional butter or pareve margarine (optional)

Cook yams until tender in boiling salted water. Drain. In food processor with metal blade in place, place half yams. Process, turning on and off rapidly, until evenly chopped, about 20 to 30 seconds. Add remaining yams, cinnamon, salt, cloves, sugar, 2 tablespoons butter or margarine, egg, cream or nondairy creamer, orange peel, and lemon peel. Process, turning on and off for about 20 seconds; then let run until mixture is smooth.

Pour into a greased 1-quart soufflé dish. If desired, sprinkle top lightly with brown sugar and dot with additional butter or margarine. Bake in a preheated 350-degree oven for 35 minutes. Serves six to eight.

PLAIN OL' YAMS

**12 medium-size sweet
potatoes**

Wash and pierce potatoes. Place in an 8-inch × 12-inch glass baking dish and cover with plastic wrap. Microwave on High for 10 minutes. Rearrange baking dish. Microwave on High for additional 12 to 14 minutes or until potatoes are fork-tender. Let stand, covered, for 5 minutes before serving. Peel and serve. Serves twelve.

SORCHÉE'S SWEET POTATO BISCUITS

**1½ cups flour
2 tbsp. light brown sugar
4 tsp. baking powder
1 tsp. salt
½ tsp. cinnamon**

**¼ tsp. nutmeg
½ cup butter
1 cup cooked sweet
  potatoes, puréed
½ cup milk**

Preheat oven to 425° F. In a large bowl, mix together flour, sugar, baking powder, salt, cinnamon, and nutmeg. Cut butter into small pieces. Stir into mixture until it resembles coarse meal. Stir in sweet potato purée and milk.

Drop batter by tablespoons on a greased baking sheet and bake for 15 minutes or until golden brown. Makes two dozen.

SOUTHLAND SWEET POTATOES

**2 lbs. sweet potatoes
¼ tsp. salt
¼ cup water
1 16-oz. can applesauce**

**⅔ cup brown sugar
2½ tbsp. butter or pareve
  margarine**

Peel sweet potatoes and slice ½ inch thick. Place salt and potatoes in a 2-quart glass casserole. Add water, cover, and cook in microwave on Medium (50 percent power) for 10 minutes. Stir lightly. Cook for 5 minutes longer on 50 percent power or until sweet potatoes are tender. Drain.

Arrange half potatoes in a 1½-quart glass casserole. Sprinkle with about 4 tablespoons brown sugar. Spoon half applesauce over potatoes and dot with 1 tablespoon butter or pareve margarine. Repeat layers. Use remaining brown sugar and butter or pareve margarine to top casserole. Cook, uncovered, on 50 percent power for 4 minutes. Place under broiler element for a few seconds for a crusty top. Serves eight.

SWEET POTATO SOUP

5 to 6 medium-size sweet potatoes
2 medium-size white potatoes
3 tbsp. pareve margarine
1 cup coarsely chopped onion
3 cups tart cooking apples, peeled, cored, and coarsely chopped (about 2 large apples)

5 10½-oz. cans kosher condensed chicken soup
4 kosher smoked sausages
2 bay leaves
1 tsp. thyme
½ tsp. pepper

Peel potatoes. Cut into 1-inch cubes. Drop into large bowl filled with cold water. Heat margarine in a large Dutch oven. Add onions and apple. Sauté about 5 minutes. Drain potatoes and add to sautéed onions and apples, stirring occasionally, cooking for about 10 minutes. Do not let vegetables brown.

Add chicken soup, sausages, bay leaves, thyme, and pepper. Heat to boiling. Reduce heat. Simmer, covered, until vegetables are tender, about 1 hour.

Remove sausages to a small bowl and reserve. Remove vegetables with slotted spoon and place in food processor. With metal blade in place, process with on and off pulses until vegetables are smooth. Return puréed vegetables to the soup and stir well.

Chop sausages and stir into soup. Blend well. Serve hot. Serves ten.

YAMBILEE FRITTERS

2 cups grated sweet
  potatoes
¼ cup all-purpose flour

¼ cup sugar
vegetable oil for frying

Wash, peel, and grate sweet potatoes. Add flour and sugar. Shape into 2-inch by ½-inch patties. Pan-fry on both sides until golden brown. Serves six.

YAMLAND MUFFINS

2 cups flour
2 tsp. baking powder
½ tsp. salt
½ tsp. nutmeg
½ tsp. cinnamon
⅓ cup seedless raisins
⅓ cup butter or margarine,
  softened

¾ cup packed brown sugar
¼ cup molasses
2 eggs, beaten
1 cup mashed cooked
  sweet potatoes
½ cup milk

Sift together flour, baking powder, salt, nutmeg, and cinnamon. Add raisins and coat with flour mixture. Cream butter or margarine, sugar, and molasses. Add beaten eggs, mashed sweet potatoes, and milk and blend well. Stir in dry ingredients, blending only until flour disappears.

Fill greased muffin pans two-thirds full. Bake at 400° F. for 20 to 25 minutes. Makes about fifteen.

YAM LATKES

2 lbs. sweet potatoes
4 tbsp. softened butter or
  pareve margarine
salt and pepper to taste
2 eggs, lightly beaten

1 large onion, finely
  chopped
2 to 3 tbsp. flour
oil for frying
applesauce (optional)

Peel sweet potatoes, cut into 1-inch thick slices, and cover with cold tap water. Bring to a boil, add salt to taste, and cover. Cook until tender, about 30 minutes.

Drain potatoes and return to pot. Mash well with butter or pareve margarine. Season with salt and pepper to taste. Add eggs and blend in. Stir in onions. Add flour.

Coat the bottom of a large frying pan with about 3 to 4 tablespoons oil and heat until moderately hot or until one drop of batter sizzles when dropped into hot oil. Drop one large serving spoon of potato purée into hot oil. See if it holds its shape. If not, add a little more flour to mixture. Fry remaining batter over moderate heat for 3 to 4 minutes each side until nicely browned, turning carefully with a spatula. Add more oil as needed with each batch. Serve with apple-sauce, if desired. Serves eight.

YAM WALDORF SALAD

8 cups diced, peeled yams
2 cups diced celery
4 cups unpeeled, diced
  apples (about 3 large
  apples)

½ cup seedless raisins
¾ cup chopped pecans
1½ cups mayonnaise
¼ tsp. nutmeg (optional)

Parboil potatoes until just tender, 3 to 5 minutes. Plunge into cold water; then drain in colander.

In a large salad bowl combine remaining ingredients. Add potatoes and toss gently until well coated with mixture. Chill for 2 to 3 hours before serving. Serves eight to ten.

YENTE'S YAM AND SAUSAGE SUPPER

6 medium sweet potatoes
1 cup applesauce
2 eggs, lightly beaten
½ tsp. salt

½ tsp. cinnamon
¼ tsp. nutmeg
12 kosher breakfast link
sausages

Combine sweet potatoes, applesauce, eggs, salt, cinnamon, and nutmeg. Mix well and pour into a greased 1½-quart casserole dish. Fry sausages until browned on both sides. Arrange sausages over yam mixture. Bake in a moderate oven (350° F.) for 30 minutes. Serves six.

Hanukah
HISTORICAL LANDMARKS

Hanukah, the Festival of Lights, celebrates the victorious battle of Judah Maccabee over the Syrian king, Antiochus, in the second century B.C. A miracle occurred at that time, when a small cruse of oil was found with which to rekindle the Eternal Light. The miracle was that the cruse of oil, which should have lasted but one day lasted for eight. To commemorate this miracle, candles are lit for each of the eight days of Hanukah. The Menorah, an eight-branched candelabra, is a major religious symbol reserved exclusively for this annual celebration of religious freedom and rededication of the ancient temple.

The house of worship, better known as a synagogue or temple, has its genesis in the first four American synagogues. These earliest synagogues have earned the status of national landmarks. As one tours the United States, the oldest synagogue in the United States is Touro Synagogue located in Newport, Rhode Island, which was dedicated in 1763. It was built by the descendants of emigrés from the Dutch colonies, Portugal, Spain, and England, who landed on those shores in the seventeenth century. Like the Acadians, these people fled to gain religious freedom, and they soon became an integral part of the growing young country. Two hundred years later, in 1963, Touro Synagogue, still with its original architectural details and artifacts, was rededicated. It is a legacy for future generations.

As one moves South, the oldest synagogue in continuous use is found in Charleston, South Carolina. K. K. Beth Elohim was dedicated in 1794. A fire in 1838 destroyed the original structure, but two years later it was rebuilt. This synagogue is recognized as the birthplace of Reform Judaism and has the distinction of being the first synagogue in this country to include instrumental music in its service. It has the international distinction of being the world's oldest surviving Reform Synagogue.

Our tour turns northward to another landmark house of worship. The Central Synagogue is the oldest Reform Congregation in New York. The synagogue was built in 1870 by the first Jew to practice architecture in America, Henry Fernbach. Its Moorish Revival and Gothic sanctuary seats more than 1,300 people.

From New York, we head toward the Midwest, where we make our last stop, in Cincinnati, Ohio. This fourth landmark is the Isaac M.

Wise Temple, named in honor of the founder of Reform Judaism in this country. It is also known as the Plum Street Temple. Built in 1865, this landmark is Moorish in style and its architecture has been equated with the flowering of Judaic culture in Spain during the Middle Ages. The word *temple* was adopted by the more liberal Reform group around the end of the nineteenth century, as opposed to the word *synagogue*, which was associated with the Orthodox house of worship. This landmark, like the other three, is open to the public for regular guided tours.

In all four landmarks, and in all synagogues and temples throughout the world today, the Menorah remains a visual symbol. As its candles are lit for eight consecutive days, that miracle of Hanukah is best expressed in Hebrew by the words handed down from generation to generation, "Nes Gadol Hayah Shem," a never-to-be-forgotten reminder that "A Great Miracle Happened Here."

HANUKAH

Cajun Chanukah Latkes *(Conventional)*
Candlelight Cupcakes *(Conventional)*
Chanukah Quik Chik *(Conventional)*
Charleston Cheese Pancakes *(Conventional)*
Collette's Cauliflower Latkes *(Conventional)*
Dreidel Custard Dessert *(Conventional)*
Festival Fruited Latkes *(Conventional)*
Hannah's Herbed Latkes *(Conventional)*
Judah's Jewish Chicken *(Conventional)*
Landmark Latkes *(Processor and Conventional)*
Menorah Fruit Salad *(Conventional)*
Menorah Vegetable Salad *(Conventional)*
Miracle Cookies *(Conventional)*
Paw's-Nip Pancakes *(Processor and Conventional)*
Plum Street Pudding *(Conventional)*
Shamus Spinach Pancakes *(Processor and Conventional)*
Shayna's Sour Cream Pancakes *(Conventional)*
Simcha Sweet Potato Pancakes *(Conventional)*
Spicy Sephardic Pancakes *(Conventional)*
Touro Tuna Latkes *(Conventional)*
Traditional Potato Latkes *(Conventional)*

CAJUN CHANUKAH LATKES

1½ cups yellow cornmeal
1 cup unsifted all-purpose
  flour
1 cup grated American
  cheese
¼ cup minced onion
2 tbsp. chopped pimento

2 tbsp. chopped green
  pepper
2 tsp. salt
½ tsp. baking soda
1 cup milk
1 egg, beaten
vegetable oil for frying

Combine cornmeal, flour, cheese, onion, pimento, green pepper, salt, and baking soda. Stir in milk and egg. Beat until blended. Drop by teaspoonfuls into deep hot fat (375° F.). Fry until golden brown on both sides. Drain on absorbent paper towel. Makes about two dozen.

CANDLELIGHT CUPCAKES

1 pkg. golden pound cake
  mix
2/3 cup water
1/2 tsp. almond extract
1 3-oz. pkg. cream cheese,
  softened
2 eggs
1/3 cup strawberry or
  raspberry preserves

2 cups powdered sugar,
  sifted
2 tbsp. milk
1 tbsp. margarine or butter,
  softened
1/4 cup sliced almonds,
  toasted

Preheat oven to 350° F. Line 18 medium (2¼-inch × 1¼-inch) muffin cups with paper baking cups. Beat dry cake mix, water, almond extract, cream cheese, and eggs on low speed of mixer, scraping bowl constantly, until moistened. Beat on medium speed, scraping bowl frequently, for 3 minutes.

Divide batter among muffin cups. Place a scant teaspoonful preserves on batter in each cup. Bake until cupcakes are golden brown and spring back when touched lightly, about 30 minutes.

Immediately remove from pan; cool. Mix powdered sugar, milk, and margarine or butter until smooth. Frost cupcakes. Sprinkle with almonds. Makes eighteen.

CHANUKAH QUIK CHIK

2 fryer chickens (about 3
  lbs. each), cut into parts
1 envelope dried kosher
  onion soup mix

1/2 cup ketchup
1/3 cup mayonnaise
1 10-oz. jar apricot
  preserves

Place chicken in a large baking pan. Combine onion soup mix, ketchup, and mayonnaise with preserves. Spoon over chicken parts. Bake in a 325-degree oven for 1¼ hours or until chicken is tender. Serves eight.

CHARLESTON CHEESE PANCAKES

1 cup cottage cheese
2 eggs, separated
1½ tbsp. cornstarch

½ tsp. sugar
¼ tsp. salt

Blend cottage cheese, egg yolks, cornstarch, sugar, and salt together. Beat egg whites until stiff and fold into cottage cheese mixture. Drop by the tablespoon onto hot, greased griddle. Lower heat and cook on one side until puffed and dry. Then turn and brown lightly on other side. Serves two.

COLLETTE'S CAULIFLOWER LATKES

1 lb. fresh cauliflower, cut up
1 tbsp. margarine
1 small onion, chopped
3 tbsp. unseasoned bread crumbs

1 egg, beaten
salt and pepper to taste
¼ tsp. chopped parsley
¼ scant cup vegetable oil

Remove stems and leaves from cauliflower. Wash and break it into flowerets. Cook in a large pan of boiling water, uncovered, on high heat for 10 to 15 minutes or until very tender.

Heat margarine in a small frying pan. Add onion and sauté over low heat for about 10 minutes or until soft and golden.

Drain cauliflower thoroughly after it is cooked. Mash with a fork until only small pieces remain. Add bread crumbs, egg, sautéed onion, and seasonings and mix well.

Heat oil in a large frying pan. Take 1 tablespoon cauliflower mixture and press it together to make it compact. Flatten into a patty about ½ inch thick. Drop into hot oil and fry until brown on each side (about 3 minutes per side). Carefully turn with a spatula. Repeat with remaining batter.

Drain latkes on paper towels. Latkes can be kept warm in a 300-degree oven with door open while you fry remaining batter. Makes about sixteen small latkes.

DREIDEL CUSTARD DESSERT

⅓ cup margarine or butter
1 pkg. golden pound cake
   mix
1 tsp. cinnamon
1 egg
¼ cup margarine or butter
3 unpared medium cooking
   apples, sliced

¼ cup honey
1 5¼-oz. pkg. kosher
   vanilla instant pudding
   and pie filling
1½ cups milk
2 cups chilled whipping
   cream

Preheat oven to 350° F. Cut ⅓ cup margarine into dry cake mix until mixture resembles cornmeal. Stir in ½ teaspoon cinnamon and egg. Press evenly in ungreased 13-inch × 9-inch × 2-inch pan. Bake until light golden brown, 15 to 20 minutes. Cool completely.

Heat ¼ cup margarine in a heavy 10-inch skillet until melted. Add apples, honey, and remaining cinnamon. Cook over medium-low heat, stirring occasionally, until apples are almost tender and sauce is thickened, about 20 minutes. Cool.

Prepare pudding and pie filling according to package directions for pudding, except decrease amount of milk to 1½ cups. Beat whipping cream in a chilled 4-quart bowl until stiff.

Fold pudding into whipped cream; pour over crust. Arrange apples on top. Drizzle with additional sauce from apples, if desired. Refrigerate until chilled, at least 1 hour. Serves about twelve.

FESTIVAL FRUITED LATKES

1 cup flour
1 tbsp. sugar
1 tbsp. baking powder
½ tsp. salt
1 cup milk
1 egg, beaten
2 tbsp. margarine, melted

1 cup shredded, peeled
   apple
1 8-oz. pkg. Philadelphia
   cream cheese, softened
½ cup sour cream
1 tbsp. sugar

Combine dry ingredients. Add milk, egg, and margarine, mixing until moist. Fold in apple. For each latke, pour 2 tablespoons batter onto hot, lightly greased griddle. Cook until surface is bubbly; turn. Continue cooking until golden brown.

Combine cream cheese, sour cream, and sugar, mixing until well blended. Serve with latkes. Makes about eighteen.

HANNAH'S HERBED LATKES

2 eggs
3 cups grated potatoes
⅓ cup grated onion
3 tbsp. flour
1½ tsp. salt

½ tsp. parsley flakes
½ tsp. rosemary leaves
¼ tsp. ground sage
¼ tsp. pepper
vegetable oil for frying

Beat eggs until light and foamy. Stir in grated potatoes, grated onion, flour, seasonings, and herbs until thoroughly blended.

Heat about ¼ inch oil in a large heavy skillet. Drop about ¼ cup potato mixture into hot oil for each latke. Fry on each side until golden brown. (You may need to add more oil to keep the oil deep enough for frying.) Drain latkes on absorbent paper towels. Makes about eighteen.

JUDAH'S JEWISH CHICKEN

1 4-lb. roasting chicken,
   cut into parts
salt and pepper to taste
1 tsp. paprika
¼ tsp. garlic salt

3 large onions, cut up
1 bay leaf
about ¼ cup ketchup

Season chicken parts with salt, pepper, paprika, and garlic salt. Arrange chicken parts in a blue granite roaster. On top add cut-up onions and bay leaf. Roast covered for ½ to ¾ hour in a 350-degree oven, until a gravy forms. Remove chicken from pan. Add to gravy enough ketchup to make a rich brownish sauce. (You may also need to add a little water.)

Remove gravy from roaster. Arrange chicken one layer deep, spooning a little gravy over each piece. Roast uncovered in a 425-degree oven until chicken turns a dark reddish-brown, about 10 to 15 minutes. Turn oven down to 300° F. and continue to heat about 15 more minutes or until chicken is fork tender. Serves four.

LANDMARK LATKES

1 egg
1 small onion, quartered
2 tbsp. matzo meal
½ tsp. salt

pepper to taste
3 medium-size potatoes,
   peeled and cubed
vegetable oil for frying

In food processor fitted with metal blade, process egg, onion, matzo meal, salt, and pepper until smooth. Add cubed potatoes. Process again until mixture is fairly smooth.

In a large skillet, heat ½ inch of oil until hot. Drop a scant ⅓ cup potato mixture into the oil several inches apart. Flatten each mound into a 4-inch circle. Fry until golden brown, turning once. Drain on paper towels. Makes about ten.

MENORAH FRUIT SALAD

¾ lb. Philadelphia cream cheese
1 16-oz. can pineapple spears

8 Maraschino cherries
½ lb. walnut halves

Cover an oval platter with a thin, smooth layer of cream cheese. On this, arrange pineapple spears to represent a Menorah with candles. To do this, across center of platter, lengthwise, place 3 pineapple spears end to end. Place 8 pineapple spears vertically on these to represent 8 candles. To form base of Menorah, place under lengthwise line of pineapple spears, in center, 2 half-pieces of pineapple, side by side vertically, and underneath these, one spear horizontally.

On top of each pineapple "candle," place a cherry for a flame. Sprinkle the walnut halves around the edges of the platter before serving. Serves about four.

MENORAH VEGETABLE SALAD

6 hard-cooked eggs
about 12 black or green
  olives
14 large, fresh-cooked or
  canned whole green
  asparagus tips

paprika

Put whites of eggs through a coarse sieve and spread solidly on a large flat platter to use as background. Lengthwise across the center of the platter place 3 pieces of asparagus, end to end. Place 8 pieces of asparagus vertically on these, to represent 8 candles. To form base of Menorah, place under lengthwise line of asparagus tips, in center, 2 half-pieces of asparagus, side by side vertically, and underneath these, 1 piece of asparagus horizontally.

Mash yolks with a little softened butter or mayonnaise and form them into tiny balls with a point at one end, to represent top of flame. Sprinkle with paprika and place above the 8 asparagus "candles." Use remainder of yolk mixture to form larger balls and place alternately with olives to form a frame around edge of platter. Serves about six.

MIRACLE COOKIES

1 cup solid vegetable
  shortening
2 cups sugar
3 eggs
1 tbsp. vanilla extract

4 cups sifted cake flour
4 tsp. baking powder
1 tsp. salt

Cream shortening and sugar together until light and fluffy. Add eggs one at a time, beating well after each addition. Stir in vanilla extract. Sift dry ingredients together 3 times. Stir into batter and blend well.

Place dough on floured board and roll out ¼ inch thick. Cut with cookie cutters into Chanukah symbols. Place cookies on greased cookie sheet. Bake in a 350-degree oven for 12 to 15 minutes. Makes about five dozen.

PAW'S-NIP PANCAKES

¾ lb. (2 to 3) parsnips, peeled
1 small baking potato, peeled
1 small tart apple
¼ cup chopped onion
⅓ cup unsifted all-purpose flour

2 large eggs, lightly beaten
1 tsp. salt
¼ tsp. pepper
¼ cup vegetable oil
¼ lb. sliced lox
1 shallot, top only
½ cup sour cream

Cut parsnips, potato, and apple to fit feed tube of food processor. With shredding blade in place, place parsnips, potato, and apple in feed tube and using slight pressure on pusher, shred vegetables. Remove from processor and place in a large bowl. Add chopped onions. Sprinkle mixture with flour and toss to coat well. Add eggs, salt, and pepper and mix well.

In a large heavy skillet, heat vegetable oil. For each pancake, drop a heaping tablespoon parsnip mixture into hot oil. With spatula or back of spoon flatten each pancake to make it about 2½ inches across. Cook for 3 minutes on each side or until golden brown and crisp.

Drain well on paper towels. Cut lox into 2½-inch × ¼-inch strips. Thinly slice top of shallot. Sprinkle shallot tops over sour cream. Before serving, place 1 tablespoon sour cream and shallot mixture on each pancake. Arrange 2 strips lox over sour cream. Serves eight.

PLUM STREET PUDDING

6 tbsp. sugar
2 tbsp. cornstarch
3 cups orange juice
2 eggs, separated
¼ tsp. almond extract

4 large oranges, peeled and
  thinly sliced
toasted, slivered almonds
  (optional)

In a medium saucepan, combine 3 tablespoons sugar with cornstarch; gradually stir in orange juice. Lightly beat egg yolks; stir into juice mixture. Stirring constantly, bring mixture to a boil over medium heat and boil for 1 minute. Remove from heat; stir in almond extract. Cool to room temperature.

In a small mixer bowl, beat egg whites until foamy. Gradually beat in remaining sugar. Beat until mixture holds soft peaks. Fold egg whites into juice mixture. Line 6 dessert glasses with orange slices. Spoon pudding into glasses. Garnish with slivered almonds, if desired. Serves six.

SHAMUS SPINACH PANCAKES

½ head lettuce
½ medium onion
2 medium potatoes
3 carrots
2 cups fresh chopped
  spinach
2 eggs, well beaten

1 cup all-purpose flour
½ tsp. salt
pepper to taste
½ pt. sour cream
4 tbsp. margarine or butter
4 tbsp. vegetable oil

With food processor fitted with metal blade, process lettuce, onion, potatoes, carrots, and spinach until smooth. Add well-beaten eggs and pulse once or twice to blend well. Remove mixture from processor to large bowl.

Sift together flour and salt and fold into vegetable mixture. Add pepper to taste.

In a large heavy skillet, heat margarine or butter and oil together. When hot, drop spinach mixture by spoonfuls into hot oil and cook until golden brown. Serve with sour cream. Serves four.

SHAYNA'S SOUR CREAM PANCAKES

4 eggs, separated
2 tbsp. sugar
1½ tsp. salt
1 cup cottage cheese,
    drained

1 cup sifted flour
½ tsp. baking soda
1 cup dairy sour cream

Beat together egg yolks, sugar, and salt until thick and light colored. Add cottage cheese and mix well. Stir together flour and baking soda. Add flour mixture in 3 additions alternately with sour cream, beginning and ending with flour mixture. Beat until smooth. Let batter stand for 10 minutes.

Beat egg whites on high speed of electric mixer until stiff peaks form when beater is lifted. Fold into batter. Using ¼-cup measure, pour batter onto hot greased griddle. Cook over medium heat until lightly browned on one side; turn and brown on other side. Makes about sixteen.

SIMCHA SWEET POTATO PANCAKES

2 cups mashed sweet
  potatoes
2 eggs
½ cup coarsely grated
  onions
4 tsp. all-purpose flour
1 tsp. ground nutmeg
1 tsp. curry powder

½ tsp. ground black pepper
½ tsp. salt
¼ tsp. cayenne pepper
8 tbsp. unsalted butter or
  margarine
8 tbsp. vegetable
  shortening

Place potatoes and eggs in a medium-size bowl. Squeeze out liquid from grated onions and add onions to bowl. Add flour, nutmeg, curry powder, pepper, salt, and cayenne pepper. Stir well. Cover and refrigerate for 1 hour before cooking.

In a medium-size nonstick pan, melt 2 tablespoons butter or margarine and 2 tablespoons vegetable shortening over medium heat. When oil begins to sizzle, drop spoonfuls of potato mixture to form pancake about ¼ inch thick and 3 inches in diameter. Brown, turn, and brown other side. Repeat until all mixture is used, adding more butter or margarine and shortening as necessary. Makes ten to twelve.

SPICY SEPHARDIC PANCAKES

3 medium potatoes, peeled
1 medium onion, finely
  chopped
3 tbsp. olive oil
1 lb. fresh spinach
3 large eggs, beaten

½ tsp. turmeric
½ tsp. cumin (optional)
1½ tsp. finely chopped
  garlic
salt and pepper to taste
vegetable oil for frying

Boil potatoes until tender; drain and mash. Sauté onion in olive oil until soft and translucent. Wash and dry spinach thoroughly, removing stems. Chop fine. Add spinach to onions and cook, stirring, for 1 to 2 minutes. Place in a large bowl and stir in remaining ingredients except vegetable oil.

Heat oil in a large frying pan. Add mixture by spoonfuls to form 3-inch pancakes. Fry until golden on both sides. Serves six to eight.

TOURO TUNA LATKES

2 cups flaked tuna fish
2 eggs
2 tsp. onion salt
6 medium potatoes, peeled
  and grated

½ cup matzo meal
vegetable oil for frying

Mix tuna fish with eggs and onion salt in a large mixing bowl. Add raw grated potatoes and mix well. Gradually mix in matzo meal. In frying pan, heat vegetable oil until hot. Drop potato mixture by the tablespoon into hot oil; fry in deep fat until crisp and golden brown on both sides. Remove and drain on paper towels. Serves six.

TRADITIONAL POTATO LATKES

6 large potatoes
2 eggs
2 tbsp. flour
1 tsp. salt

pepper to taste
1 small onion, grated
¼ tsp. baking powder
vegetable oil for frying

Grate potatoes and drain. Add remaining ingredients except vegetable oil and mix well. Drop by tablespoonfuls into hot oil at least ¼ inch deep. Fry until brown on both sides, turning only once so that pancakes do not get soggy. Serves six.

Potpourri
A LITTLE BIT OF THIS
AND A LITTLE BIT OF THAT

POTPOURRI
(A Little Bit of This, and a Little Bit of That)

Breads

Beersheba Biscuits *(Conventional)*
Beulah's Banana Nut Bread *(Conventional)*
Catahoula Corn Bread *(Processor and Conventional)*
Comeaux's Corn Bread *(Microwave)*
Perli's Praline Bread *(Conventional)*
Plaquemine Pumpkin Bread *(Conventional)*
Pointe à la Hache Pumpkin Bread *(Microwave)*
Pointe Coupée Challah *(Processor and Conventional)*
Rifke's Rice Corn Bread *(Conventional)*

Beverages

Cold Eggnog *(Conventional)*
Hot Eggnog *(Microwave)*

Eggs

Cicely's Cornmeal Crepes *(Conventional)*
Edie's Egg Loaf *(Conventional)*
French Toast à l'Orange *(Conventional)*
Garlic en Grits *(Conventional)*
Lite and Airy Egg Custard *(Microwave and Conventional)*
Panéed Pancakes *(Conventional)*
Patty's Pickled Eggs *(Conventional)*

Relishes

Crispy Zucchini Pickles *(Conventional)*
Eula's Eggplant Relish *(Conventional)*
Peachy Pickles *(Microwave and Conventional)*
Potpourri Relish *(Conventional)*
Reuben's Red and Green Pepper Relish
        (Microwave and Conventional)

BEERSHEBA BISCUITS

1 cup vegetable shortening
5 cups flour
1½ tsp. baking soda
5 tsp. baking powder

3 tbsp. sugar
1 pkg. dry yeast
5 tbsp. warm water
2 cups buttermilk

In a 3-quart mixing bowl combine flour, baking soda, baking powder, and sugar. Cut in shortening. In a 1-quart mixing bowl, dissolve yeast in warm water and add buttermilk. Add to dry ingredients and mix until well blended. Dough will be soft and slightly sticky.

Turn onto a well-floured cloth or board. Sprinkle with flour and knead gently for about 30 seconds. Roll and cut into biscuits. Place on greased cookie sheet and cover with towel. Let rise in a warm place for about 30 minutes. Bake in a preheated 400-degree oven for 15 minutes or until golden brown. Makes four to five dozen.

BEULAH'S BANANA NUT BREAD

½ cup butter or margarine
1 cup sugar
2 eggs
2 cups flour
1 tsp. baking soda

½ tsp. salt
1 cup mashed bananas
   (about 3 medium
   bananas)
½ cup chopped pecans

Cream butter and sugar thoroughly. Add eggs, beating until blended. Sift together flour, baking soda, and salt. Add to beaten mixture; then blend in bananas and nuts. Spread mixture in a greased 9-inch × 5-inch loaf pan. Bake in a 350-degree oven for 1 hour or until toothpick inserted in center comes out clean. Cool on a wire rack before removing from pan. Makes one loaf.

CATAHOULA CORN BREAD

1 cup flour
1 cup yellow cornmeal
1 tbsp. baking powder
1 tsp. salt

½ cup butter, cut into
  pieces
1 cup milk
2 eggs

In food processor with metal blade in place, place flour, cornmeal, baking powder, salt, and butter. Process until butter is completely cut into flour mixture, about 20 seconds. Continue to process while pouring milk through feed tube all at once. Add eggs one at a time, processing until mixture is well blended. Pour batter into a buttered 8-inch × 8-inch × 2-inch pan and bake in a preheated 400-degree oven for 25 to 30 minutes. Cut into squares when cool. Serves nine.

COMEAUX'S CORN BREAD

1 cup flour
1 cup yellow cornmeal
4 tsp. baking powder
¾ tsp. salt
2 tbsp. sugar (optional)

2 eggs
1 cup milk
¼ cup cooking oil
1 tbsp. butter or margarine

In a 2-quart bowl, combine flour, cornmeal, baking powder, salt, and sugar if used. Mix well. Add eggs, milk, and oil and stir until well blended. Preheat microwave browning skillet on High for 5 minutes. Butter preheated skillet and pour in batter.

Microwave on Medium (50 percent power) for 7 to 9 minutes or until middle of bread is set and no longer shakes. Microwave on High for 2 to 3 minutes or until toothpick inserted in center comes out clean. Allow to stand for 5 minutes before turning out onto platter. When cool, cut into squares. Serves nine.

PERLI'S PRALINE BREAD

1 cup chopped pecans
1 cup Praline Liqueur
1 cup butter
1 tbsp. vanilla extract
2 cups tightly packed dark
  brown sugar

5 eggs
¼ cup milk
2 cups all-purpose flour
1 tsp. cinnamon
½ tsp. baking powder

Marinate pecans in ⅓ cup Praline Liqueur for 1 hour. Cream together butter, vanilla, and sugar in a large mixing bowl. Add eggs and milk. Sift flour, cinnamon, and baking powder into mixture. Add pecans and liqueur.

Pour into 2 greased 5-inch × 9-inch loaf pans. Bake in a preheated 300-degree oven for 60 to 70 minutes. Cool on racks. When completely cool, pour ⅓ cup liqueur over each loaf. Wrap loaves in foil and let stand at least 3 hours before serving. Makes two loaves.

PLAQUEMINE PUMPKIN BREAD

2 cups sifted all-purpose
  flour
2 tsp. baking powder
½ tsp. baking soda
1 tsp. salt
1 tsp. cinnamon
½ tsp. nutmeg

1 cup solid-packed
  pumpkin
1 cup sugar
½ cup milk
2 eggs
¼ cup softened butter
1 cup chopped pecans

Sift together flour, baking powder, baking soda, salt, cinnamon, and nutmeg. Combine pumpkin, sugar, milk, and eggs in a large mixing bowl. Add dry sifted ingredients and butter and mix until well blended.

Stir in pecans. Spread batter in a well-greased 9-inch × 5-inch × 3-inch loaf pan. Bake in a 350-degree oven for 45 to 50 minutes or until a toothpick inserted in center comes out clean. Makes one loaf.

POINTE À LA HACHE
PUMPKIN BREAD

1½ cups all-purpose flour
1½ cups sugar
1 tsp. baking soda
¾ tsp. salt
½ tsp. nutmeg
½ tsp. cinnamon
8 oz. canned pumpkin,
   mashed

2 eggs, beaten
1 tsp. vanilla
½ cup vegetable oil
⅓ cup water
¾ cup chopped pecans

In a 2-quart bowl, combine flour, sugar, baking soda, salt, nutmeg, and cinnamon. Mix well. Add mashed pumpkin, eggs, vanilla, oil, and water. Mix well. Stir in nuts. Pour into microwave bundt pan or glass loaf pan.

Microwave on Medium (50 percent power) for 18 to 20 minutes or until center is set and no longer shakes. Microwave on High for 4 to 5 minutes or until a toothpick inserted near center comes out clean. Let stand for 2 minutes before turning out. Serves ten to twelve.

POINTE COUPÉE CHALLAH

2½ tsp. dry yeast
1 tbsp. sugar
¼ cup warm water (105 to
   115° F.)
2¾ cups all-purpose flour
1 tsp. salt
1 tbsp. pareve margarine

1 egg
½ cup water
vegetable oil
1 egg yolk
2 tbsp. cold water
poppy seeds (optional)

Stir yeast and sugar into warm water and let stand until bubbly (5 to 10 minutes). In food processor with metal blade fitted, place flour, salt, and margarine and process for 10 seconds. Pour egg and yeast mixture down feed tube and process for 10 seconds.

With the machine running, slowly pour just enough water down feed tube so that mixture forms a ball of dough on blades and leaves side of work bowl clean. Process ball of dough for 15 seconds. Slowly add just enough of remaining water to make dough soft, smooth, and satiny but not sticky. Process for another 10 to 15 seconds.

Oil your hands, shape dough into a ball, and place dough in a greased bowl, turning to grease all sides. Cover loosely with plastic wrap and let stand in a warm place (80° F.) until doubled (about 1 hour). Punch down dough, divide into 3 equal parts, and shape each part into a 24-inch-long strand. Braid strands loosely together. Tuck ends under and pinch to seal.

Place braid on a greased cookie sheet, brush with vegetable oil, and let stand in a warm place until almost doubled (about 45 minutes). Preheat oven to 375° F. Beat egg yolk and cold water together and brush mixture over braid. Sprinkle with poppy seeds, if desired.

Bake until evenly browned, about 25 to 30 minutes. Remove from cookie sheet and cool on a wire rack. Makes one large loaf.

RIFKE'S RICE CORN BREAD

1 cup yellow cornmeal
1 cup white cornmeal
1 tsp. salt
1 tsp. baking soda
2½ tsp. double-acting
  baking powder
1 tbsp. unsalted butter,
  softened

1 tbsp. sugar
1 cup cooked rice, cooled
  to room temperature
3 large eggs, beaten lightly
2 cups buttermilk

In a large mixing bowl, combine yellow cornmeal, white cornmeal, salt, baking soda, and baking powder. In a separate large bowl stir together butter and sugar. Add rice, mashing it slightly, and mix well. Stir in eggs and buttermilk, mixing well. Add cornmeal mixture and stir batter until it is just combined. Spoon batter into a buttered 8-inch-square cake pan and bake in a preheated 400-degree oven for 30 to 35 minutes or until a toothpick inserted in center comes out clean. Cool bread in pan on a rack for 10 minutes. Cut into squares. Serves six to eight.

COLD EGGNOG

6 eggs, separated
¾ cup sugar
1 oz. rum

1 qt. half-and-half
1 pt. bourbon
grated nutmeg

In a large bowl, beat egg whites until foamy. Slowly add ¼ cup sugar and beat until whites are very stiff.

In a separate bowl, beat egg yolks with ½ cup sugar until thick and lemon colored. Fold egg whites into egg yolks; then fold in rum. Stir in half-and-half and bourbon. Serve very cold with grated nutmeg sprinkled on top. Makes approximately 1½ quarts.

HOT EGGNOG

1 qt. milk
4 egg yolks
⅓ cup sugar
¼ tsp. cinnamon

¼ tsp. nutmeg
¼ tsp. vanilla extract
2 cups sherry (optional)

Heat milk in microwave in a 2-quart glass dish or casserole for 5 minutes on 50 percent power. Beat egg yolks lightly with sugar, spices, and vanilla. Stir about 1 cup hot milk into egg mixture. Then gradually blend all of yolk mixture into milk. Cook on 50 percent power for 5 minutes. Stir halfway through cooking time. Stir in sherry before serving. Makes 1½ quarts.

CICELY'S CORNMEAL CREPES

¾ cup yellow cornmeal
¼ cup flour
2 eggs
¼ cup canned cream-style
  corn

½ cup milk
2 egg whites
¼ cup melted butter, plus
  butter for greasing skillet

Sift together cornmeal and flour and set aside. In a large mixing bowl, beat whole eggs well. Add corn and milk and beat to blend. Add cornmeal mixture and beat thoroughly.

In a separate bowl, beat egg whites until stiff and fold into batter. Fold in melted butter.

Heat a griddle or skillet and brush lightly with melted butter. Pour about 2 tablespoons batter at a time onto the griddle and cook until crepes are nicely browned on one side. Turn and cook about 1 minute on the other side or until crepes are cooked through. Makes about eighteen.

EDIE'S EGG LOAF

**1 loaf French bread (about
    12 inches long)
8 eggs
¼ cup milk
⅛ tsp. Tabasco sauce**

**2 tbsp. butter or margarine
¼ lb. sharp cheddar
    cheese, shredded
1 tbsp. chopped chives**

Preheat oven to 400° F.

Cut off one end of French bread and set aside. Hollow out loaf, leaving a shell about ¾ inch thick. In a large bowl, beat eggs, milk, and Tabasco sauce until well mixed. In a large skillet over medium heat melt butter or margarine. When it is hot, add egg mixture and cook until eggs are set but still very moist. Stir in cheese and chives.

Remove skillet from heat. Spoon egg mixture into bread shell, replace end, pressing tightly to hold it in place. Place filled loaf on a cookie sheet. Bake 10 minutes or until heated through. Cut into 1-inch-thick slices and serve hot. Serves four.

FRENCH TOAST À L'ORANGE

2 eggs, beaten
½ cup orange juice
1 to 2 tbsp. honey
¼ tsp. vanilla extract

4 slices bread
butter or margarine for
  greasing skillet

Mix together eggs, orange juice, honey, and vanilla. Dip bread slices into mixture. Fry in lightly buttered skillet for about 3 minutes on each side or until nicely browned. Serves two.

GARLIC EN GRITS

1 cup 5-minute grits
4 cups water
1 tsp. salt
4 cloves garlic, minced

6 strips Beef Frye
8 eggs
1 stick pareve margarine
salt and pepper to taste

Cook grits in water seasoned with 1 teaspoon salt for 5 minutes. Add minced garlic and stir well. Fry Beef Frye slices until crisp; crumble and set aside. Fry eggs in ½ stick pareve margarine until cooked to your taste.

Place grits on four serving plates. Top with pat of pareve margarine, sprinkle with crumbled Beef Frye, and top with two eggs. Add salt and pepper to taste. Serves four.

LITE AND AIRY EGG CUSTARD

2½ cups milk for
  microwave or 3 cups milk
  for conventional method
4 eggs

½ cup sugar
⅛ tsp. salt
1 tsp. vanilla
nutmeg

MICROWAVE: Place milk in a 4-cup glass measure. Cover tightly with plastic wrap, turning back edge to vent. Microwave on 100 percent power for 4 to 5 minutes or until steaming hot. Beat eggs, sugar, and salt together. Gradually beat in hot milk. Stir in vanilla. Pour into a 4-cup microwave-safe ring mold. Microwave on 50 percent power for 7 minutes, stirring twice. Stir well and sprinkle with nutmeg. Microwave on 50 percent power for 3 to 5 minutes longer or until custard is nearly set. Rotate ring mold every minute. Remove from oven and cover with plastic wrap. Cool for 30 minutes. Chill well before serving. Serves six.

CONVENTIONAL: Lightly butter a 1-quart casserole or ring mold. Preheat oven to 300° F. Heat 3 cups milk in a saucepan over low heat until tiny bubbles form around edge. Stir often to prevent skin from forming on top of milk. Beat eggs, sugar, and salt together. Gradually beat in hot milk. Stir in vanilla. Pour into prepared dish. Sprinkle with nutmeg. Place in larger baking dish and add boiling water to come halfway up side of dish.

Bake for 1 hour and 15 minutes or until knife inserted in custard comes out clean. Remove custard from water bath and cool on wire rack. Chill well before serving. Serves six.

PANÉED PANCAKES

1 cup all-purpose flour	2 tbsp. melted butter
2 tsp. baking powder	2 eggs, well beaten
1 tbsp. sugar	¾ cup half-and-half
½ tsp. salt	

Mix flour, baking powder, sugar, and salt together. Add melted butter and beaten eggs to half-and-half. Mix well. Add dry ingredients to egg mixture and stir just enough to distribute evenly. Batter will be slightly lumpy. Drop batter by the tablespoon onto hot greased griddle. When edges begin to bubble and are slightly brown, flip over and brown other side. Serve with additional melted butter and syrup or preserves of your choice. Serves two to four.

PATTY'S PICKLED EGGS

12 hard-cooked eggs
2 cups vinegar
1 cup water
2 tbsp. sugar
1 tsp. salt
½ tsp. celery seed

1 tsp. mixed pickling
  spices
salt, black pepper, and
  cayenne pepper to taste
1 clove garlic, minced

Simmer vinegar, water, sugar, salt, celery seed, pickling spices, garlic, and additional salt, black pepper, and cayenne pepper in a large pot. Cool liquid. Shell eggs and put in a large jar or crock. Strain liquid over eggs and seal tightly. Store in refrigerator for 2 to 3 days before serving. Makes twelve.

CRISPY ZUCCHINI PICKLES

5 lbs. zucchini, thinly
  sliced
3 medium onions, thinly
  sliced
½ cup salt
ice cubes
3 cups white vinegar

3 cups sugar
2 tsp. celery seed
2 tsp. mustard seed
1½ tsp. turmeric
1 tsp. ginger
½ tsp. pepper

Combine zucchini, onions, and salt in a bowl. Top with layer of ice cubes. Cover and let stand for 3 hours. Drain and rinse zucchini and onions in cold water. Combine zucchini mixture with vinegar, sugar, celery seed, mustard seed, turmeric, ginger, and pepper in a large kettle. Heat to boiling; reduce heat and simmer for 2 minutes.

Ladle into pint jars and seal. Process in boiling water at simmering temperature for 10 minutes. Makes six pints.

EULA'S EGGPLANT RELISH

2 medium eggplants, cubed
3 tbsp. salt
⅓ cup olive oil
½ cup chopped onions
⅓ cup shallots
3 cloves garlic, minced
¼ cup chopped parsley

1 8-oz. can tomato sauce
2 small or 1 medium
   tomato, chopped
¼ cup vinegar
1 tbsp. sugar
⅛ tsp. black pepper
⅛ tsp. cayenne pepper

Put eggplant in a bowl, sprinkle with salt, and let stand for a couple of hours.

Drain. Sauté eggplant in olive oil and remove from skillet. Sauté onions, shallots, garlic, and parsley until vegetables are limp and transparent. Add eggplant and remaining ingredients. Cover and simmer slowly about 10 minutes, stirring occasionally.

Pack into hot jars, seal, and process in hot water bath for 20 minutes. Makes five to six half-pints.

PEACHY PICKLES

½ cup cider vinegar
⅓ cup sugar
¼ tsp. ginger
1 stick cinnamon

6 whole cloves or ⅛ tsp.
   ground cloves
3 large peaches, peeled and
   quartered

MICROWAVE: Combine vinegar, sugar, ginger, cinnamon, and cloves in a 2-quart glass bowl or casserole. Cover tightly with plastic wrap, turning back edge to vent. Microwave on 100 percent power for 4 minutes or until sugar dissolves, stirring twice. Add peaches and stir to coat. Cover, leaving vent, and microwave on 100 percent power for 6 minutes, stirring once. Let stand for 30 minutes before serving. May be served warm or chilled. Serves six.

CONVENTIONAL: Combine vinegar, sugar, ginger, cinnamon, and cloves in a saucepan. Heat to boiling. Reduce heat, cover, and simmer for 5 minutes. Add peaches, cover, and simmer for 10 minutes or until peaches are tender. Let stand for 30 minutes before serving. May be served warm or chilled. Serves six.

POTPOURRI RELISH

1 16-oz. pkg. cranberries	1 apple
1 orange	1¼ cups sugar

Wash fruit. Remove seeds from orange and core from apple. Grind cranberries with other fruit (skins included). Stir in sugar. Spoon into a 1-quart container and seal. Keep in refrigerator until ready to use. Makes one quart.

REUBEN'S RED AND GREEN PEPPER RELISH

2 small sweet red peppers, seeded and diced	½ cup vinegar
2 small sweet green peppers, seeded and diced	¼ cup sugar
	½ tsp. salt
	¼ tsp. crushed red pepper
1 onion, chopped	1 bay leaf

MICROWAVE: Combine all ingredients in a 2-quart glass bowl or casserole. Stir until well mixed. Cover tightly with plastic wrap, turning back edge to vent. Microwave on 100 percent power for 5 minutes. Stir well. Cover, leaving vent, and microwave at 70 percent power for 10 minutes longer, stirring twice. Let stand, covered, for 5 minutes. Remove bay leaf, stir, and chill. Makes 2¼ cups.

CONVENTIONAL: Combine all ingredients in a large saucepan. Heat gently to boiling, stirring occasionally. Reduce heat, cover, and simmer for 30 minutes longer, stirring occasionally. Remove bay leaf, stir, and chill. Makes 2¼ cups.

Bon Voyage

One would think the Cajun people and the Jewish people would be worlds apart. Strangely, however, their backgrounds, their ideals, their customs, and even their cuisines share a common bond.

The Cajuns left their homeland seeking freedom from oppression. They traveled from France to the New World, first to Canada then to Louisiana. The Jews came to the New World from all four corners of the earth, settling in large cities and small towns throughout the United States. Both peoples brought with them skill, ambition, and determination. Both built homes for themselves in a strange new land, all the while retaining their old-world traditions, their strong family ties, and their culinary heritage. The Cajun and Jewish cultures have lived on; the people persevered and survived by adjusting to their new surroundings and the opportunities that prevailed, whether in the community or in the kitchen. Both delight in sharing with you their heritage and their unique cuisine.

We have concluded a tour of Cajun country that has been not only picturesque but also tasty. Along the way we have stopped to savor some kosher holiday fare and to show you the connection between the Cajun and Jewish cultures. We have blended the best of both worlds to offer you Kosher Cajun cooking. In sharing this cuisine with you, we hope you will find it "quelque chose piquante" (something spicy), "quelque chose de doux" (something sweet) from the Cajun kitchen and "Oy! Iz dus a mechaieh" (Oh, is this delicious!), "takka zeir gut" (it's really very good) from the kosher kitchen.

Au revoir and shalom!

Glossary

Acadiana: Area in south Louisiana settled by the Cajuns.

Acadians: Original inhabitants of Acadiana, nicknamed Cajuns by Indians in the region.

Adlayodah: An indoor carnival celebrated during Purim.

Alligator: Cajun yard dog.

Allons manger: Let's eat.

Allons à Thibodaux: Come on to Thibodaux.

Ashkenazim: Jews of Central and Eastern European origin.

Au revoir: Farewell, goodbye.

Bayou: A sluggish stream, bigger than a creek and smaller than a river.

Beef Frye: Kosher sliced cured smoked plated beef.

Beignet: Doughnut without a hole.

Bienvenu: Welcome.

Bisque: A thick, rich cream soup usually made with seafood or puréed vegetables.

Blanc: White.

Bon bouche: "Good mouthful," something you save for the last delicious bite.

Bonjour: Cajun greeting, "hello."

Bon temps: Good time.

Bon voyage: Farewell; have a good trip.

Boucherie: A slaughter, butchering.

Bouillabaisse: A highly seasoned stew made of two or more kinds of fish, sometimes seasoned with wine.

Bubbie: Jewish grandmother.

Buccaneer: A pirate.

Café: Coffee.

Cajun: Descendant of French colonists exiled from Nova Scotia who settled in south Louisiana.

Cajun cooking: Simple, hearty, spicy cooking developed by the Cajun people.

Cantor: Trained professional singer who assists the Rabbi in religious services.

Carnival: Any merrymaking, usually noisy; a costumed revelry.

C'est bon: It is good.

Chang-a-lang: Musical triangle.

Chanukah: See *Hanukah.*

Chari vari: A noisy ritual performed for newlywed widows or widowers. Tin pans are beaten, cowbells rung, etc. to create as much noise as possible.

Coq au vin: Chicken in wine.

Coup de main: To give a hand; assist.

Courtbouillon: Fish stew made with tomato sauce.

Crepe: Thin pancake.

Croquette: A small patty of mashed foods, usually dipped in bread crumbs and fried.

Davener: A person in prayer.

Diaspora: The body of Jewish people living outside the State of Israel.

Dreidel: Toy top used to play Hanukah games.

Eppes Essen: Something to eat.

Eternal Light: The ever-burning light above the Holy Ark.

Etouffée: Smothered.

Fais do do: Literally "go to sleep," also a Cajun social gathering.

Fiddlers: Cajun musicians of string instruments.

Filé: Powdered sassafras leaves used to thicken gumbo.

Fillet: To remove bones from fish; boneless strips of fish.

Fritters: Batter containing fruit or other ingredients, dropped in deep fat or sautéed.

Gabbai: Jewish sexton.

Ganza megillah: A very long story.

Gefilte fish: A combination of various fish, chopped or ground, usually served as an appetizer.

Glacé (or glazé): Glazed, as with a very thin frosting.

Grandpère: French and Cajun grandfather.
Gumbo: Thick, savory soup made with fowl or seafood.

Hamantaschen: Three-cornered filled pastry baked only for Purim.
Hanukah: Jewish eight-day Festival of Lights.
Hollandaise: Yellow egg sauce with seasoning.
Hutzpah: Nerve; gall. Same as Chutzpah.

Jambalaya: Dish made from rice combined with seafood, meat, or
     fowl.
Joie de vivre: Joy of life.

Kashruth: Jewish dietary laws.
Kibbutz: Cooperative settlement of farmers in Israel.
Kosher: Foods adhering to Jewish dietary laws.
Kreplach: Noodle dough filled with meat, usually dropped in soup-
     like dumpling.

La bonne cuisine: The good cooking.
Lafourche: "The fork."
Laissez les bon temps rouler: Let the good times roll.
La poussière: The dust.
Latke: Potato pancake.
Le bon changement: A good change.

Megillah: The long story read on Purim; Scroll of Esther.
Menorah: Eight-branched candelabra.
Mirliton: Pear-shaped vegetable in squash family.
Mon cher: My dear.
Moshav: Collective farm settlement in Israel.

Nahit: Chick peas; garbanzo peas.
Nes gadol hayah shem: A great miracle happened here.
Noir: Black.

Oy! Iz dus a mechaieh: Oh, is this delicious!

Panéed: Pan fried.

Pareve: Foods that may be served with either milk or meat dishes.
Parlons français ici: Speak French here.
Paté: Paste or spread.
Paysan: Countryman.
Pelican: Cajun eagle; also Louisiana state bird.
Petit: Small, tiny.
Pilaf: Rice with seasoning.
Piquante: Sharp and spicy.
Pirogue: Cajun canoe, originally made from dug-out cypress log.
Potpourri: A miscellaneous collection.
Poulet: Chicken.
Praline: A sweet treat made with sugar and pecans.
Purim: Holiday commemorating the Jewish victory over the Persian
    plot to exterminate the Jews.

Quelque chose de doux: Something sweet.
Quelque chose piquante: Something spicy.

Rebbitzen: Wife of a Rabbi.
Remoulade: Sauce of spices and seasoning used over seafood.
Roux: Basic mixture of flour and shortening used as thickening
    agent; pronounced "roo."

Schvarzadick: Blackened.
Sephardic: Jews of Spanish and Middle Eastern origin.
Shallot: Green onion; interchangeable with scallion.
Shalom: Hebrew all-purpose greeting for hello, goodbye, peace.
Shamus: Caretaker of the Synagogue.
Simcha: Happy occasion.
Sucre: Sweet, sugary.
Synagogue: Jewish Orthodox House of Worship.

Tabasco: Hot pepper sauce.
Takka zeir gut: It's really good.
Tante: Aunt.
Temple: Jewish Reform House of Worship.
Très bon: Very good.

Tzadek: A righteous and holy man.
Tzibel: Jewish for onion.

Vinaigrette: Sauce made with vinegar, oil, and seasoning.
Vise-ah: White.
Vorscht un luckshen: Sausage and spaghetti.

Yam: Southern sweet potato.
Yente: Busybody.

Zayde: Jewish grandfather.

Index

Processor Index

Microwave Index